# The Best of Wanderlust Journal 2019

*EDITED BY*

M. Brianna Stallings
Sarah Leamy

Wild Dog Press,
PO Box 836,
Cerrillos, NM 87010
www.wilddogpress.org

# THANK YOU

This anthology grew out of the overwhelming support and global interest in www.wanderlust-journal.com. As readers looking for a wide variety of travel writing, we have to search numerous individual blogs or read blogs focused on promoting a specific destination. *Wanderlust* is the only one-stop resource for numerous writers to share their personal experiences out in the world. Together we're building an international community, with contributors to the site from 64 countries, readers from 114, and over 56,000 site views in the first year.

Explore. Share. Inspire.

# CONTENTS

# 1. Is this the End of the World?

**James Agombar**

*Savai'i, Western Samoa*

I knew it would be memorable part of my trip, but this underestimation made me question a few things.

The boat from Upolu was soothing and people mostly kept their heads down to thwart the sea-sickness. At the dock I checked the map and started walking what I thought was north to the hostel to check for vacancies, but I had lost all sense of direction by then. A man in a truck gave me a ride before I got one hundred paces down the crumbly road.

He dropped me off at Lusia's, which had been recommended. The fale' was luxury; a small bamboo shelter with shutters for windows and private mosquito net. Even better was that the other bed was vacant. The sun went down, the ocean lapped small crabs and fish into the cove by my fale', and the bar was open; paradise had been found.

The next day paradise took a chicane or two, as did I. I had taken a walk through Salelologa to a local car hire garage in order to get to the far side of the island and reach my destination. Unfortunately, businesses, houses and sometimes derelicts can look deceptively similar. I found the sign for the car rental place which was on the far side of the forecourt and I walked down the grass alley near the sign. I ended up in front of someone's house. It didn't look like anyone was home, but the five dogs were, and they were raging that I had intruded as far as I had. Realizing my mistake, I turned and started walking away, briskly. I heard the huff of the approaching dogs behind me and the pack leader wrapped its jaws around my right ankle and slipped off as I pulled it forward. My leg went numb and I went down to one knee. As I looked up, the dogs had me surrounded, and all I could think was to clench my fists to try and fight them off. Then a saviour came in the form of a rock. A small boy was home, no older than nine, who started pelting them with rocks and shouting. The boy ran over to me and helped me up as the dogs retreated to the house. He didn't speak a word of English but I could tell he was very sympathetic toward me. Sometimes heroes came in the most unexpected form.

By then the man from the car rental place had seen what happened and ran over. He helped me limp to his office. He sat me down and put my bloody foot into a ice cream tub full of dirty salt water and the feeling came back in the form of a sting.

He hired me a car and I drove myself to hospital in a 1.2 automatic Toyota as the only ambulance on the island had been out of service for some time. I pulled up outside after eleven kilometers and tried not to bleed over the footwell. I limped in and signed up. An old lady with an eye-patch stood up to let me sit down on one of the stone benches. I felt terrible. After an hour I was patched up by a Samoan nurse and a doctor from New Zealand. My tendon was actually hanging out the back of the knick in my ankle. Luckily, Rabies hadn't been introduced to the island and he prescribed me some painkillers after covering it with antiseptic. He told me to take it easy, that I was very lucky and let the nurse patch me up. I tilted my head back in pain as she placed the bandages which caused my sunglasses to slip off my bandana straight into a bin full of bloody rags. I said she could keep them.

Common sense told me I should go back to the fale' and rest. Determination said I should soldier on and reach my goal. Guess which one I listened to?

I continued along the road to the other side of the island, going easy on the accelerator. After civilisation became more basic, it became more beautiful.

The trees to my left were strewn amongst the chasms and curves in the landscape. They appeared so thick with flora it was like they had been draped with pond weed. To my right was the coast line, reflecting a beautiful glow in my wing mirrors. The road was thin and damaged in so many places that it became a task of full concentration. The tendon at the back of my ankle didn't help the journey. It started to bleed through the bandage, and the smell of the iodine patch underneath reminded me of the dog racing up to bite it. Despite being eager to reach my destination, I eased off the accelerator even more, knowing it was very close. The morning rain had caused steam to rise from the trees when the intense sun just started to peak. As I drove slowly on, the thick jungle started to fray and the lava fields of western Savai'i came into view. The greenery started to increase in terms of hue and texture whilst the branches of more scattered trees became sparse. A wire fence caught my eye where someone had erected a sign saying "NO TRESPASSING — RESTRICTED AREA — KEEP OUT," in large letters. I pulled over and hung out of the car door for a moment to feel the thick atmosphere on me like a blanket of sweat. To stay in an air conditioned vehicle for this journey seemed to nullify the whole attraction of this holy area. I climbed back in, cancelled the air-con and opened the windows fully. A few miles meandered through quiet villages of traditional bamboo and fishing territory before I reached an opening to Falealupo Peninsula, otherwise known as "the end of the world."

The coastline sand started to turn black, producing smooth rocks. Seeing a woman in the distance on the road, I slowed to ask her how close I was. She wore a bright red and orange lava-lava (sarong) and carried a basket of fruit.

"Talofa! Excuse me, can you tell me if the end of the world is close?" I asked, slowly.

She smiled in reply and surprised me with fluent English, "Ah, not long now, maybe another kilometer or so for you," she gestured down the road.

The road meandered, and a burnt out vehicle appeared to the far left. It had been caught in the lava fields; left to rust as a relic of nature's power over man and machinery.

It was when the radio in the car began to transmit white noise that I knew I was close. Radio transmissions didn't reach out this far from the mainland.

The coastline soon became solid rock, but the colours developed a contrast. Pulling over, I stepped out inspecting the rocks more closely to greet the sound of the crashing ocean, the taste of salty air and the cushion of golden, spongy sand. I limped forward with my right leg now dragging. The pain enhanced as the blood circulated. The nerves in my ankle itched and writhed across the skin like snakes on a lake. With a creased brow and clenched fists I carried on, knowing I was too close to stop.

A tattoo-covered Samoan man in a traditional lavalava came to my aid on the beach and introduced himself to me as David.

"Is this the end of the world?" I asked him, as he put his arm around my waist to support me.

"Yes. You are here," he replied in his best English. "Do you need help to cross?"

"Please," I assented, and he walked me across to the rocks.

We stepped onto the volcanic rock, dark and smooth as before, but now scattered with white pebbles. The pebbles were then dashed with crimson specks of coral, much like bloodstains. The wind grew stronger here, relieving the sweaty blanket of salty air, and the tide splashed against the formation I stood on with ethereal effect.

David helped me to where the ocean sprayed us as it bounded off the rocks. In front of us there was a large X in white, possibly chalk, on a large surface of rock. It marked the end of the world and the last piece of land on Earth to see the sun. To cross the date line on the Pacific would throw you twenty-seven hours ahead in time. On the edge of the last time zone, I stood with David and gazed upon the endless, refreshing ocean. Taking a deep lungful of frenetic air, I smiled, knowing I had made it to where the spirits of Samoa gathered: Falealupo Peninsula, the end of the world.

# 2. No Problem

**Susan Aspley**

*Thailand, 1990*

After the all night train ride, I arrive in Bangkok at oh-dark-thirty.

I rub my eyes, yawn, and immediately light a cigarette, along with most of the train car of travelers.

A few minutes later, a train attendant comes with a tray of half filled, half warm, murky glasses of thick coffee. "You, ten baht," he says, smiling too brightly at this hour.

"No, five baht," I answer.

"No, no, ten baht. You."

I give him ten baht, too tired to argue, while the rest of the Thais around me pay him the five baht. At least the man across from me, who was incredibly smashed last night, looks more tired than I. He stares at some uncertain spot, his head bobbing like a cheap doll.

The air is tolerably cool and lightly damp before the city of Bangkok fully wakes. Eerie and hopeful. We chug slowly across an iron bridge just as the sun shows its first peachy glow. Lining the tracks live a world of squalid and chattering slum people.

Too much in too little space, rammed together, tight as a brick wall. Laundry swings out every window, hairless dogs, grimy kids, noodle stands, boiling woks, garbage, garbage, garbage.

The dwellers squat and stare as the train rumbles through their front yard.

I sit quietly and stare back at them, wondering what they are thinking as they watch the train pass by.

We slowly wind between the dawning city and end up at the central station. The train lurches into the depot like a drunk stumbling home, fourteen hours after departing Nakorn Sri

Thammarat, my southern home in Thailand during my Peace Corps years.

Once the train lurches to a shaky standstill, it dry heaves, gasps for breath, then pukes out the passengers stuffed inside.

When I step off the train, a stub of a man with no legs frog hops up to me, his knuckles looking like calloused elephant paws. He is level to my knees, with a greasy New York Yankees baseball cap, no shirt, and shorts tied with rubber bands at the bottom to hold in his stumps. He sits in front of me and holds his hands in a pathetic wai.

If I can spend ten baht on nasty coffee, I can surely give him ten baht also. So I give him twenty. He pockets the money, wai's and scoots away.

I'm then harassed by taxi car drivers.

"Get away from me," I grouch, and head for a tuk tuk parked nearby.

Tuk tuks are Bangkok's notorious three-wheeled motorized rickshaws. "Tuk tuk" translates as simply the sound it makes. The proper name for these are sam laws (three wheels).

They are demon chariots. Acid trip carnival rides, racing through the mad circus traffic of Bangkok. They are Fun. Dangerous. Efficient.

I always smell like exhaust afterwards and my hair is a mess, but they are quicker than a city bus and cheaper than a taxi car.

After bargaining with the driver over price, we agree on something reasonable — still overpriced, but not outrageous.

Feeling adventurous, I decide to stay in a part of the city I've never explored before, only passed through. It's an upscale shopping haven, drawing the wealthiest of tourists and foreigners. I am not meeting Beth and Clare until tomorrow on the other side of town, so have the day and night to myself.

I arrive at Sukhumvit Road, and wander around looking for a place to stay. I decide on a little boutique hotel. I check in and plan to enjoy every inch of the heavenly carpet, sacred air conditioning and blessed real bed.

My dad always told me, "Sue, you are my favorite daughter." (I'm his only daughter.) I would always answer, "Dad, you are my favorite dad." So my favorite dad had sent me, his favorite daughter, twenty dollars a week for a very long time which I saved, and this room is where much of that money is going.

After a long, cool tub bath, the first bathtub bath I've had in almost a year, I lounge around my glorious hotel room, feeling like a queen.

The next indulgence is breakfast down the street at a fancy five star hotel a real bakery. I spend exactly twenty times the amount that I would normally spend in Nakorn for a meal. I order fresh bread rolls with real butter, caramel cheesecake, a toasted, buttered bagel with cream cheese and a kid's grilled cheese sandwich.

On the way back to my room, stuffed, I realize I left the bulk of my money in my fanny pack on the bed in the hotel.

How the hell could I forget that? How? I never take that thing off unless I shower. I don't have it, it's back at the room. I panic.

Oh, no.

Oh, no, no...


A feeling crawls over me like ten thousand slow leeches. Once in my room, I have a meltdown. The money belt is here, but the money's gone. I wail like a bereaved Muslim mother and run down to the reception desk. The maids and the desk clerk look at me cautiously, slyly, but not surprised or concerned. I blubber in broken Thai sobs that someone stole my money from my room. Then I run back to my room, search again desperately, and return to the desk.

It's gone. I'm berserk.

The clerk responds coldly and becomes defensive. She tells me specifically that I lost the money outside and no one stole it. She denies that anyone at the hotel stole it, that something must be wrong with me. I never accused her or the maids of anything. I only said the money was stolen, could have been another guest.

Her vibes are negative and black. The anger inside me wads into a tightly packed knot. I tell her I need to check out because I have no money and want my room charge and deposit back. She shakes her head, no, and I start crying. She remains hard as a rock. I plead. I beg. I wait. She starts to curse at me. I resort to calling her nasty names in English. She calls me nasty names in Thai. I think briefly about calling the police, but know what little help that would do.

I have no proof. When it's a Thai against a foreigner in a situation such as this, nothing is done. Thais win. Foreigners are told to go home. I have no proof.

Within about one minute, I grab my backpack and am out on the street hailing a real taxi cab. I'm bawling, and even though I had already paid for the room, plus a deposit, there is no way I want to stay. I just want to leave.

I jump into the first taxi without bargaining as I scrounge up enough words to get me to the other side of this massive city. Hopefully, the Peace Corps office is open and I can get my per diem money right away.

The old driver never takes his eyes off me in the rear-view mirror except to quickly glance at the road.

"Why are you sad?" he asks.

"Because I hate Thailand. Fuck Thailand. I am so stupid," I mutter back.

"What happened?"

"They stole my money. I know they went into my room and took my money. I am so stupid. They knew I would be stupid."

I continue to stare at the broken door handle for the hour ride through traffic, wishing my dad was here to help me.

The driver starts speaking gently in Thai. I don't understand half the words he is saying. I am too upset to process much of anything.

At the landmark where I told him I wanted to go, he pulls over. I get out, dig through my purse and find my last fifty baht to pay the fare. Definitely not enough to cover what it should really cost, but all I have left.

I hand it to him.

He nods, smiles and pulls off, disappearing into the jam of cars and smog.

I am left still holding my fifty baht bill. Humbled.

# 3. The Clandestine Chef

**Anthony Bain**

*Barcelona, Spain*

Deep in the heart of central Barcelona, I step into an apartment building entranceway. The décor instantly grabs my attention, created when the city experienced a metamorphosis of modernist architecture; intricate multi-colored murals look down at me from high ceilings. It's an awe-inspiring sight, designed to disarm any visitor. For a second, I cannot believe I have the right place, nothing indicates that a social event is in full swing, there are no lights, no muffled conversations, and no scent of cooking seeping out into the stone corridor; only silence, the flickering of defective strip lights, and the musty, humid smell of the apartment foyer.

I follow a winding staircase up to the first floor and knock on a large wood paneled door and hear the knocking reverberate beyond the door and into the next space, which seems vast and expansive. I stand for a moment, reading from a crumpled paper in my hand to make sure that I haven't stumbled across the wrong address. The door opens, I suddenly feel like a tourist exiting a plane in a strange and mysterious land, exotic aromas spill out into the stairway; the compression chamber is open. I have finally arrived.

Using the same approach as the supper clubs of the Jazz days of post-prohibition America, Mount Lavinia is a clandestine restaurant, moving from basement flat to art loft, to kitchen space. Keeping the concept of exotic gastronomy fresh and on the move throughout a city well-known for its gastronomic prowess. For a long time, I have yearned to take my taste buds on a journey. Not just dine out at a restaurant and order an exotic meal, but to live the experience and have the chef explain every intricate detail of what goes into the preparation of the food, from market to table. Total immersion dining.

Chef Faraaj, the creator of Mount Lavinia Supper Club, hands me an imported Lion beer and shows me towards a group of eight people who are circulating around a work surface and an open chill out area. They talk amongst themselves, while he carefully blends spices in a stone mortar and pestle and hands out titbits on the history of Sri Lanka and the spice trade.

"It's based on quite a few periods of colonization." He says, constantly picking up jars from his work surface, measuring spices hand to eye, and adding them to a pot which has already begun to sizzle on the hob. "It's a blend of indigenous ingredients and local cooking techniques with influences from Portuguese, Indonesian, and Malay cooking."

I ask him about the idea behind Mount Lavinia Supper club.

"In one word; disillusionment," he says, sighing in obvious frustration. "Asian food in this city tends to be modified or diluted to the Spanish palette. I want to give Barcelona authentic Sri Lankan cuisine as you would eat it in anybody's house in Sri Lanka without compromising on taste."

As an entrée, Chef Faaraj rolls mango slices covered in grated coconut, sprinkled with lime juice and a bit of chili powder for "a kick," to wake up the taste buds and hands them out to his guests along with fresh tuna and black pepper croquettes and Okra Samosas.

Two foodies from New York introduce themselves to me and intensely discuss the quality and flavors of the food while Chef Faaraj dispenses another round of Lion beer to his guests. He then gets down to work on the main course, dhal, a lentil dish which he adds the array of pre-blended spices to, he then turns his attention to a large bowl of basmati rice seasoned with finely crushed cardamom and coriander seeds and cashew nuts.

The rest of the guests chill out in the apartment lounge where a Sri Lankan travel documentary silently plays on a projector while Asian hip-hop spills out from a sound system. The whole setup is designed to whet the guest's appetite and give an encompassing feeling of being in-country and clandestinely traveling via the senses.

I ask Chef Faaraj if he's ever thought of opening his own restaurant.

"I could never open my own restaurant," he says surprised by my question. "I need to be able to shop and cook the food personally. That way I know what I'm serving. I have one hundred percent quality control on everything, something which I would risk by opening a commercial enterprise. Cooking for me is like painting a picture. I could never allow anybody else to pick up the paints and easel and takeover."

He tells me that all of his ingredients are sourced from La Boqueria, Barcelona´s famous food market and every local chef's favorite hangout, where food is shipped in daily from all over the world. Every ingredient he meticulously researches to keep the menus as "Sri Lankan as possible." Preparation and execution from the market to table are profoundly personal things to him.

Several of the guests have now migrated towards Faaraj who is busy slicing locally farmed marbled beef to create a beef curry, he warns us that "the curry might be spicy," but encourages us to sip the fruity Lion dark beer to "chase the spice," and, "bring out the flavors."

While he is busy adding the beef to a sizzling pan, he tells us stories about how his family prepares dishes back in Sri Lanka. By now all the guests are around the kitchen central table unit and carefully listening to him. Some of them are returning guests. "He changes the dishes, every month," they whisper to me, careful not to interrupt the chef in mid flow. "One month it's seafood, the next it's street food, and sometimes he does Sri Lankan tapas." It's clearly the innovation and variation of the chef's food that keeps them coming back.

Two of the guests are French chefs who are doing a clandestine restaurant tour of Barcelona, to see for themselves the frontier of culinary exploration. They behave like two children in a sweet shop, wide-eyed, in awe of their surroundings. "People are becoming more adventurous," they tell me. "They no longer conform to the normal dining standards, they want to be more involved in the process and interact with the chef on a personal basis, the clandestine restaurant allows them to do that."

Clandestine restaurants also offer a promising chef a way to evolve and grow without the make or break pressure of opening a restaurant. The idea of the clandestine restaurant´s secrecy means that it attracts like-minded people, who seek something more intrepid and more tangible. Reservations are made via social networking websites. The whole social concept of the clandestine restaurant is a natural extension of social media; previous guests can invite friends, the experience works to perfection in Barcelona, a social, culinary hub continually renewing itself and pushing the boundaries of modern cuisine, pioneered by vanguard chefs like Albert Adria and Joan Roca.

Chef Faaraj announces that dinner is ready and all the guests take a seat at the table and immediately tuck into the food set out like a banquet on the work surface. We dine on Roti pancakes, succulent beef curry with potatoes, rice with cashews, dahl with coconut cream, fried okra with green chilies and Pol Sambol: a coconut and red chili accompanying dish.

As the guests begin to devour the food, a silence falls across the table which is eventually shattered by Chef Faaraj, he shrugs his shoulders and starts to belly laugh, this breaks the ice and the conversation around the table takes off from there. The evening shifts into the later hours of the night as the guests share travel stories and food secrets around the table.

After we have all enjoyed several courses and several beers somebody suggests that we watch the documentary projected on the chill out room wall. With desserts and sweet coffee we settle in for the viewing, all us sharing the same encompassing feeling; as if we are in Sri Lanka.

Later, led by Chef Faaraj we spill out into the boulevards of Barcelona, many of us didn´t know each other before the dinner, but we have become a tight-knit group, with food secrets shared within the safe environment of The Mount Lavinia Supper Club. We've confessed our culinary sins to each other and it has brought us closer together than we could ever have imagined. The Chef leads us like a beacon into the night as we head off into a labyrinth of Gothic streets to experience what the city can offer in the way of underground experiences. Giving secret passwords to gain entry into oak paneled cocktails bars, ushered into back rooms by stern men in black uniforms, where famous cocktail waiters present gin tastings to members of secret tasting societies. Later, giddy with intrigue we slide past the queue into the VIP room of a velvet decorated discotheque, still riding on the shared experience, a rite of passage into Barcelona's clandestine world.

# 4. Being There

**Michelle Bracken**

*California, Summer, 1998*

We had never gone away together, never taken a vacation. My mother had always been too busy cleaning houses, changing diapers, and dating worthless men. But she made time, one summer when I was fourteen going on fifteen, for us to go somewhere. and To escape our everyday drudgery among cacti and overwhelming heat. It would be my mother, my five-year-old sister, and me. We were leaving for sunny Monterey and didn't know when we'd be back. I hoped never.

She drove our new used rust colored Chevy Caprice 1988 station wagon for the first time that morning. I packed the wagon with everything I thought we'd ever need: bright colored tank tops, jean shorts, beach sweaters, beef jerky and Pepsi, books (I was engrossed in Stephen King's *The Dark Half*), maxi pads (I expected my period) and music to get us by for weeks even though we'd be gone for less than one.

My mother, thin and blonde, smiled her toothy grin as she buckled her seat belt. "Ready?" she had asked. I looked at our home, large and looming in our small desert town just outside of Joshua Tree, removed from everyone and everything, and nodded.

My sister, thin and blonde like my mother, sat in the back with coloring books and crayons. She didn't bother us. Wouldn't bother us. I sat shotgun with my collection of tapes. I had organized them that week prior as if I was being graded by some god of music. I had wanted to impress my mother, impress anyone who would have heard John Lennon crooning while our windows were rolled down.

"Put that in," my mother said, nodding toward my lap. He was sitting there. John. I can't remember now the first song that we played, but at this moment I can hear the lyrics to John's rendition of "Stand by Me" and remember how I told my mother it would be a good song to ice skate to, how it rocked and rolled, how it thumped and shook.

"For her," I said, nodding towards my sister. "She could skate to this, it'd be perfect." My sister couldn't ice skate, had never seen an ice rink, but my mother and I would watch the ice skaters in the Olympics and imagine that my mother's mini-me would one day skate on that ice and make us proud. "Yeah," she smiled, "it's a good one."

The scenery all looked the same. I was used to the emptiness of the desert, to the blue sky that housed no clouds. I was used to the freeways, to the dirtiness of the freeway cities, and to the brown filth that city people called sky. I was used to all of that.

We talked about John, my mother and I. We talked about when he died and how it was weird that I was born the year he was killed and that maybe it meant something, maybe we were connected somehow, me and John, and that's why I was so drawn to him and his music and his politics and how even I loved Yoko. My mother never made me feel stupid or obsessed or insane. She never corrected me, never told me that I was born two years after he was murdered.I smiled and felt that my mother understood me. I turned and peered at the back seat. My sister had fallen asleep with a blue crayon held tightly in her little fingers.

We reached Bakersfield a day later. Yellow hills, too dry for grass, bordered us on that empty highway, freeway, whatever way that took us there. The windows were rolled way down, had been that way since the air conditioner broke the day before. The heat made me thirsty and nauseous.

We stopped at the first diner we saw. I rushed to the bathroom; my stomach had been hurting and I knew why. It was that time.

"It's my period," I groaned, sitting at the plastic red booth. The sweaty undersides of my thighs stuck to the seat as I tried to make myself more comfortable.

"Sorry, hun," my mother said. "Maybe you should get a salad or some soup. Something light." She brushed her blonde hair from her tanned face and then did the same to my sister.

I tried to eat some vegetable soup but the tomato broth made me think too much of the blood gushing between my legs and I had to think of good thoughts, of the Tejano singer, Selena, singing "Bidi Bidi Bum Bum" so that I wouldn't spew my insides all over the table.

We got back on the road.

"We'll stop in the city," my mother said, "We'll find a room and then you can take a hot bath." She patted my thigh. My sister reached over the front seat and handed me a thin piece of paper: a bear in a polka dot dress. She had stayed in the lines, the browns and purples never crossed paths.


Before we got a room, the wagon overheated.

"Turn on the heater," my mother directed.

I didn't ask questions. Did as I was told. My insides felt twisted, and the heat only made it worse. I didn't think we'd make it anywhere.

"Where to stop? Where to stop?" my mother muttered, smoke billowing from the engine.

We passed Walmart, KMart, liquor stores and green trees that I had never seen and didn't know what to call them. I still don't.

"Henry's!" she yelled out.

I followed her gaze and saw Henry's in bright green lettering; the mechanic's shop was dark and dirty, grease rubbed all over.

She parked where she could, and Henry came out to meet us. He was a giant of a man, maybe in his late sixties, with a gray, unruly beard that sprouted all over his face. My mother sent me across the busy street with my sister, her little fingers wrapped around my own.

I looked across the way and saw a museum, not one I wanted to visit. It looked more like a park, and it boasted the first homes and buildings erected in Bakersfield before it was Bakersfield. They were in prime condition, 18 something-something style. There would be no air conditioning, no haven from the heat.

But my mother gave me ten bucks, so we did the tour. My sister and I had wanted to go inside but couldn't, weren't allowed to. We looked through windows and studied the porcelain figures that someone had set up to look like people from the past.

"I wanna touch 'em!" she cried, her little hands wrapped around the golden doorknob of the first dentist office.

"Let go!" I yelled, my arms around her waist.

She kicked and screamed.

I took her outside of the entrance, where we sat on wet grass. It wasn't long before she wanted our mother.

"I'm going!" she had pouted, running for the busy street.

I ran after her, grabbed her, and told her that it was our job to stay where we were, to protect the people in those houses. This would stop her for a bit, and then she would try again for the street. I could see all too clearly her mangled body, covered in blood, crushed beneath Toyotas and Fords. I saw that for an hour, two hours, maybe three. Saw that every time I raced after her.

The sun was no longer over us when our mother returned. It was cooler, my cramps had subsided, and the sky had turned pink. My little sister saw her first, saw her cross the street and wave.

"Look! Mom!" she had yelled, giddy with anticipation. She took off, her blonde hair bounced behind her.

I got to my feet and followed.

"Ready to go?" my mother said, "I didn't think he'd do it, but he did."

"Did what?" I knew nothing of cars. Would never know anything of cars.

"The radiator had a big, gaping hole in it. All fixed now." She smiled and I took her hand.

We ran across the street.

Henry sat on a red crate, playing with his massive beard.

"My girls, the ones I was telling you about," my mother said, presenting us.

I smiled awkwardly, my sister posed faithfully. Henry gave a warm smile and stood to shake our hands. I looked at the grease on his fat fingers and pondered whether I would be disrespectful. I shook his hand.

"I'd like to sing you all a song," he said.

We followed him to a small room, off in the corner, watched him duck his head as he entered. He pulled up a worn-out wooden chair that squeaked underneath him.

I stood in the doorway and watched and listened as he played his acoustic guitar. Observed every movement he made, every note he uttered. He sang of a woman in a green dress. I didn't see an old man on an old chair, and I didn't see myself standing in a hot, stuffy room. I saw an older gentleman sitting on a park bench in the middle of spring with daisies in his hands, asking the lady beside him if she'd like to go out for dinner sometime.

When Henry finished, we all clapped and smiled, cooed how good it was. Well, my sister and my mother did that. I smiled and clapped.

Henry wiped his eyes.

We left Bakersfield in the morning. And she couldn't stop talking about him, how sweet his song was.

"Wouldn't that be it?" my mother asked, looking at me.

"Be what?"

"Everything. He's the sweetest guy I've ever met."

Then she looked ahead, continued driving, and didn't say anything more until we reached Monterey.

We went on our journey. We went along the water, along Pacific Coast Highway. We shivered at the ocean breeze (the desert heat had spoiled us), we laughed at the seagulls and how they crapped on rich people's cars, we collected rocks and seashells, got sand in our underwear, in between our toes, wore sweaters while we sunbathed, while we read books under the sun, and ate bean burritos at Taco Bell because that's what my mother did when she was fourteen going on fifteen at the beach.

I played Marvin Gaye on our way home. I sang along to every song, pictured my sister skating to "I Heard it Through the Grapevine" and "Inner City Blues." She sat in the back, drank all the Pepsi, colored more pictures of bears in dresses, and ordered every seven minutes that we stop so she could pee.

I wanted to savor those moments, driving in and out of tight curves, seeing so much green that I swore my sister had been there earlier with her crayons. I treasured being cold at the beach, even though it was summer, and I treasured sitting in that big hulk of a car, listening to my mother hum with Marvin and talk about the time she was seventeen and camped at some beach with marshmallows and pot because that's what kids did then. Maybe they still do, she had said.

My mother still has that station wagon. Still drives it. Everyday. Everywhere. The air conditioner still doesn't work and the windows are never rolled down because they can never be rolled back up. We've talked about going other places. And sometimes to the same places, maybe see Henry — but we never make plans. But there are days, nights — when I think of that summer, fourteen going on fifteen. I see my mother, clapping her hands as Henry sings, clapping her hands as if he's the only thing left in the world to clap for. I wonder if she ever claps like that anymore.

# 5. Fire

**Steve Brouillette**

*The West, USA*

You have a task, requiring an immediate decision. How you engage is going to determine action and comes with its own parameters. There's more traffic than the Tac can handle. It's no longer organized chaos. It's out of hand, but not unmanageable. You wait, poised to be direct, watching the winds, listening to what fire is telling you. It's no different, the message, once you understand. You're respectful to the way it needs to live. How it consumes, and breathes. And you wait for the wind, shifting in the pulses of breathing fire, down the flank and at the head. The aircrafts are inbound and the timing: critical. The moment you waited for is coming down the line; a shifting wind taming the flame back on itself. You go with purpose and caution held in both hands, but the wave has a crest and the ride is on. You pick your point of initial piercing and cut the volume in two, circle back from the black and hit the flank cutting off the head. While you engage the body headed to the mass in front of you, the VLATs come over the rise and drape the fuels in crimson towards the head. Others held in the rear, now go mobile to join the consumption like piranhas eating the last bits of flame and ember. But it's not enough and the fire rises in fresh wind and unchecked fuel. You've been flanked because others were too afraid to move forward. But you circle and reposition under the new-found rally, inspired. The second time, with incorporated forces common to the way, another line is drawn and cut in between the breath of winds, smoke, and heat. She's corralled and slowly consuming the last traces of a life born from spark.

# 6. Cinerama

**Danny Burdet**

*Los Angeles, USA*

If you find yourself in Los Angeles with no more pressing decisions than where you shall take your first meal of the day, which film you will see and where… if you are the beneficiary of this unaccountable good fortune, you should probably escape the force field of your reasonably comfortable bed and do as much as you can with the day.

So you trail along the controlled jungle of your motel's courtyard, various of the guests placed about a metal patio table or contentedly prostrate in pool deck chairs beneath the strengthening sun. You pass through the vestibule of this establishment that could write pulp novels with what it has seen and emerge through the establishment's curiously plantation-like facade — the face whitewashed, a broad expanse of porch and a row of imposing, unfluted columns. Into the Los Angeles morning! Well, the late morning at least.

You emerge from the Hollywood and Vine Metro station and decide as the day's voyage is beginning you will seek augury in the stars set into the walkway beneath your feet. This is all very exciting, but then the first star you espy whose name is spelled in gold within its pink star (it's like the whole thing was designed by somebody moonlighting from Frederick's of Hollywood) is Reese Witherspoon. You mean no disrespect to Ms. Witherspoon, but this is not quite the answer you were seeking in these stars. So you decide the next, yes the next star on which you focus will be the one. And sure enough, the next tacky pink star on which your eyes alight is that of good old Joe

Mankiewicz. And you think, now we're talking. But then some time later your feet fall upon the star bestowed upon that cinematic giant, Bobby Flay. Perhaps this particular set of tea leaves should be the subject of a factory recall.

Down Hollywood Boulevard, you settle on an a Middle Eastern restaurant. As many, Jonathan Gold preeminent among them, have pointed out, numerous of the city's culinary delights are hidden in plain, banal sight in its strip malls. So it is at this joint, probably not quite distinguished enough for dear departed Mr. Gold, but who knows; the man got around. Amongst all the movie popcorn, the gallons of soda and the seamy late-night fast food runs, you realize it's probably a good idea to occasionally throw your body a curve and deliver unto it a plate heaped with organic matter. Not just chicken shawarma, not just hummus and actual lettuce, but even little stalks of beets. Beets, for heaven's sake! You imagine an internal food monitor, generally inured to the flow of manufactured food and drink, practically startled out of his little chair at this unorthodox repast. Speaking in even, Spock-like tones, he says, "It would seem to be organic matter, but we can't be sure. Let us hope for the best." And indeed, you all have a lovely meal.

Sunset Boulevard is just a few blocks south on Vine, and yonder to the west is the unmistakable shape of the Cinerama Dome. You've never been, and this is to be the day. They're playing Wonder Woman in the dome because, well, everyone is playing *Wonder Woman* just now. So once more unto the breach with Ms. Gadot you will go.

But you've got time prior to the next cinema bum afternoon screening, so you wander around Hollywood along the streets mainly south of Sunset. Moving west along De Longpre (which makes you happy just to say), you come to the bland police station at Wilcox. Across the street, predictably enough, is a bail bond establishment, perhaps several under one flat roof. This low-slung building, is a riot of old signs and enticements, extending above that flat roof and painted on its facade. Perhaps the strangest bit of juxtaposition here, considering form and function, is not the almost cheerful cacophony of the signs, but the row of Christmas lights hung along the eaves of the building.

Through the relative hush of this residential area, you also see examples of Los Angeles street signs you have never quite noticed before. This the generation that first appeared in the 1940s, with its no-nonsense, "just the facts ma'am" sans serif font on a navy blue field, called the shotgun sign, much as they remind you more of a hand with an extended index finger.

These neighborhood streets are rich with expansive flowering shrubs and trees, behind which can be found lovely, modest houses. These are mainly enviable bungalows, flatter than their Chicago brethren and sheathed in wood planks instead of brick. The attractiveness and variety of these bungalows sing a seductive song with which the Midwest bungalow can't quite compete; so it goes with the West Coast. The most encouraging thing here is scale. The size of the average North American dwelling (and this definitely includes our seemingly more civilized neighbors to the north in Canada) has increased radically since the mid-20th century. But here are houses low to the ground, not far removed from the street, modest in scale. Just a few feet from the next house. It all seems very civilized. But how one affords such civilization you still don't entirely understand.

They run a tight ship at the Cinerama Dome. A squad of polite young men sell you your ticket and offer directions around the corner to the dome proper. There, another well-groomed fellow, apparently the only one on duty at this modern cathedral of cinema, drawn from the very small screen of his smart phone to take your ticket, sell you the requisite vat of diet soda and manage to say without any apparent irony, "Enjoy *Wonder Woman*."

Cinerama was originally a method of shooting and projecting film, three cameras or projectors at once. Just one of the salvos of the movie industry in the 1950s, desperate to compete with the insurgent threat of television. The triple film process was soon abandoned for the highly impractical method it was, but

70mm films were projected onto the originally 146 degree curve of Cinerama screens (not a continuous strip, but a series of narrow vertical strips carefully angled at the audience). There were once Cinerama theaters all over the world, purpose-built and adapted. Only a few remain, the Cinerama Dome (among the late, geodesic dome iterations of the chain) among them.

Even with the pre-film walk, you have arrived some 25 minutes before film time, which makes you the only person in the dome when you step through one of its side curtains. How can this be? At this famous place, in the middle of Hollywood? You have never understood the reluctance of your fellow man and woman to "leave the warm precincts of the cheerful day" in favor of a darkened theater, but it takes all kinds. So, you have the Cinerama Dome to yourself for a full 10 minutes until another sole male arrives (at which time you wonder, as he might well of you: A mere cinephile? Devotee of old theaters? *Wonder Woman* fetishist? Maybe all of the above?).

Eventually, about a dozen curious souls choose to shun the California sunshine in favor of the dark of the cinema. One of those polite young men comes out, mic in hand, prior to feature time and welcomes you to the Cinerama Dome.

And then, once more all the spectacle of *Wonder Woman*. This is the second time you have seen the entertaining if not terribly complex film. But if you can exit a theater of a summer's day after seeing one of these superhero extravaganzas without a splitting existential ice cream headache, you probably shouldn't complain.

You'd thought you would just stick around for a while, enjoy the theater experience and then leave before *Wonder Woman* sprawled to the conclusion of its 141 minutes. But to your surprise, you stay until the victorious end. That Gal Gadot does light up a screen, be it Cinerama or something more humble.

You had walked around Hollywood earlier in the afternoon and thought about the wealth and the striving. You had noticed the banners hung from the poles of street lights asking for the consideration of Emmy voters in making their nominations. You had sat in this theater and considered the pressure to fill such places. Box office numbers pored over like holy writs. And well, you really like looking at Gal Gadot. Just as you were expected to in the calculus of movie capitalism. And you do anyway. So that was fun.

Not so far away up on Hollywood Boulevard is the venerable little watering hole The Frolic Room. And it would be a sin not to stop by for a drink or two on your way back to the motel. So once more out of the sun and into the shadows.

The relative hush of late afternoon is either a really sad or satisfying hour in which to do your drinking, sometimes both. The small room of the Frolic is not overrun as it can be of a night. There's a few young men at the far end of the establishment making the scene a little too loudly, as such young men are wont to do. Otherwise, it's a few guys spaced around the nearside curve of the bar, a woman sitting near the entrance against the opposite wall, not drinking as yet, and our bartender.

The young woman tending bar is slight of stature, cute in her square-framed glasses a bit incongruous relative to her scrappier wardrobe and short, slightly spiky hair. She hovers back and forth warmly and not without grace. The woman near the entrance has a slightly awkward though friendly introduction to a man who arrives, after having asked a previous patron if he was the man for whom she was waiting. Ah, the blind date. The somewhat eager, halting conversation is quite familiar in its attempt to settle into comforting rhythm. Fare thee well, would-be lovers.

You regard yourself in the mirror behind the bar. This is not always the most satisfying of exercises, but you're not entirely displeased with what you see. And there is the mere fact of this reflection.

Some six or seven months previous, you had lain on an operating table for about six hours, heart stopped. One leaky little heart valve stitched back into compliance. Another far more leaky valve replaced with something mechanical, leaving you with a pronounced tick as that heart beats. Which it does, sewn back up as you were and dispatched like an automobile with a new carburetor.

Strange things, these wonders and banalities and striving. And what mad luxury to ruminate on it all over a beer in a Hollywood bar of a late afternoon, when this is but one of many choices at your feet. A second round seems appropriate. You summon that charming bartender. That California sun will wait.

# 7. Taipei Streets (with a Japanese Eye)

**Kaori Fujimoto**

*Taiwan*

You wake up to the pattering of rain against the windows. It is June, the rainy season, the month of rat-colored skies when humidity alternates with a chill in the Japanese archipelago, your homeland. I need a vacation, you think. In Taiwan.

Why Taiwan? Because you are tired and want easy, stress-free, and cheap travel abroad. The three-and-a-half-hour direct flights between Tokyo and Taipei cost only about 30,000 yen (about 300 US dollars). None of your friends who visited Taiwan fumed over tourists' misfortune, while people have told you how they got ripped off in other neighboring countries. You lived and traveled in North America and Europe in your youth and you've been itching for your first foray into Asia outside of Japan. Above all, the name "Taiwan" inexplicably resonates deep within you.

The following week, you sit in an airport shuttle bound for the heart of Taipei, breathing in the pungent smell that recalls Chinatown, and gazing through the windows at the massive charcoal and ginger colored buildings along the highway blurred in polluted air. The substantial quality of these constructions — apparently condominiums — creates the illusion that you are on a continent, rather than an island far smaller than Japan. Probably because the Taiwanese are of Chinese origin, you speculate, as you keep inhaling the peculiar smell filling the bus. This smell — a mixture of fish, oil, spice, and other mysterious odors — grows overpowering as you exit the shuttle to walk to your hotel. Along the street, a sea of Chinese characters in solid crimson, indigo, and ivory on sooty facades stretches in all directions, illuminated by the champagne sunlight after a late-afternoon shower. Many of these buildings have a run-down look that gives the impression of unlivable apartment complexes. Your eyes continue to scour the blocks and you spot what look like traditional street eateries on which hip cafés and restaurants muscle in. Throw your baggage into the hotel and come, they beckon.

You step into an old-style eatery with a roof and no front walls. A man fries rice noodles on a sizable griddle and women serve customers. One of the servers speaks to you in Japanese, which astonishes you because she was so quick to tell that you — a woman who looks as East Asian as she is — are an alien. You are also confused because your default language outside Japan is English, so you hear yourself stuttering in English and then Japanese. She leads you to one of the sidewalk tables, and, because there is no menu, you are immediately served a bowl of spicy soup with chicken dumplings, shiitake, daikon, and cilantro, and a plate of equally hot rice noodles mixed with ground pork. A family of four takes an adjoining table, and you think that, with this substantial yummy meal costing only three bucks, you wouldn't bother to cook at home. An older woman ladles additional soup into your nearly-empty bowl. It begins to rain, then comes a tropical downpour. No one seems to notice the drumming on the eaves and splashes on the road just a yard away from their sandaled feet.

Next day, a blazing sun converts the soaked city into a steamer. Drenched with sweat, you drift onto the grounds of the historic Longshan Temple and amble through the roofed passage around the courtyard. People in their everyday clothes or black robes sit or stand randomly in the sun to chant a sutra, never minding the heat. More people stream in, holding incense sticks that look giant compared to their counterparts for Buddhist rituals in Japan where, with rare exceptions, only monks chant sutras. They place these sticks on the ash in the burners, and some of them amble across the courtyard into the building at the end of the passage. Inside the building, under rows of vermillion paper lanterns, silence reigns, and the unceasing chant outside sounds as if it were coming from behind clouds.

The chanting still echoes in your ears when you get back on the street. There, in contrast to the local Buddhists' vigorous voices and to your general impression that Chinese-speaking people have boisterous exchanges, no one talks loudly. When on the phone, many cup one hand over their mouths, like people in Tokyo do to spare strangers from overhearing their conversations. So, what prevails in the streets is never the locals' chatter but that pungent smell which grows sharper or fainter in the subtropical heat while you saunter past food markets, stalls and eateries. Sheaves of whole raw fish and squids lie limp in rows; bagged trotters' split ends point toward you or the sky; skewered chicken and pork are piled high like pyramids pierced all over with arrows; vivid-colored slices of mango, cantaloupes, pineapple and berries entice you to buy them by the bucket. At semi-open air diners, the locals eat from bowls brimming with minced pork, omelets crowned with thick amber-colored sauce, or mounds of shaved ice doused in bright orange syrup. You don't travel for food — in fact, you catch a whiff of shallowness, greed even, in people who go overseas to insatiably pursue local foods for "cultural experiences." That said, when your stomach growls, you get pulled into a classical local food court like a lassoed animal.

There, you find yourself lost among the cluster of stalls, gawking and frowning at the menus overhead. You recognize many of the letters because you know 2,000-plus Chinese characters used in Japanese, but most of these familiar logograms make no sense when combined in Chinese ways. You decipher "beef noodles," "seafood rice porridge," and "chicken thigh and rice." But what are "flower branch rice porridge," "purple leaf egg flower hot water," or "fried sewage water"? Finally, you beckon a girl working at one of the stalls. With English words and gestures, you communicate that you want to take out the second item from the left on the menu (chicken thigh and rice), and the girl hands you the food in a package with a Chinese adage printed on it: "Know you have enough; Don't deplete your good fortune." While you savor every mouthful in your hotel's quiet and air-conditioned lobby, a young employee sits near you to have his meal, watching Pokemon in Japanese on his iPhone.

Your street food experience in Taiwan climaxes at a night market, just as all travel guides guarantee. You join the hordes of people filing toward the Shilin Night Market, and soon see stuffed animals and plastic masks of anime characters, shooting games, clothing, shoes, iced tea stands, and an ocean of food stalls. You buy a cup of rice noodle soup and eat it on a stone step at a temple behind the stall, watching the endless currents of people this market attracts every night, seven days a week. You get iced café latte with black tapioca pearls crowding the bottom of the cup, and notice the sign you decode as "a small intestine wrapped in a large intestine." Of course, you try this hotdog-like food with an herbal smell that fills you enough to mark the end of your eating spree. Then you let yourself be carried in the torrent of people cascading down a staircase to the basement, and there, you witness heaven.

No floating angels or celestial light, but the locals cramming around tables to bite into fried meat or seafood, and food sellers frantically flipping omelets or stirring noodles on griddles under fluorescent lights. From the focused yet relaxed look on their faces, you can tell these people are fully there to make or eat the food, letting nothing else matter in this moment. They fill the basement with these vibes of the simple and intense mindfulness that you never thought possible in a packed food court. You watch them spellbound because they look so alive. And happy.

During the rest of your stay, you visit a peaceful, verdant quarter that features museums away from the street bustle. You watch the Changing of the Guard in Freedom Square. The grand architecture of the theater, concert hall, and memorial hall in the vast Square again makes you feel the air of a continent in this island nation. And you see enough neat-looking apartment complexes, some of which have plants and flowers growing beautifully over the iron gratings covering the windows, as opposed to those sooty buildings that struck you on your first day as barely livable.

Decoding menus remains a struggle, though you have successfully deciphered many simple public signs such as 洗手間 (restroom; 御手洗 in Japanese), 公用電話 (public phone; 公衆電話), and 天雨路滑 (the floor is slippery because of rain; 雨で足元が滑ります). This is the type of fun never available in the West.

Now you are on the boardwalk through the mangrove swamps in the northern part of Taipei, and find the quiet you wanted before flying back to Tokyo tomorrow. The sky is clear. The sun is blazing down. Cicadas are singing. Mountains and shiny modern buildings soar beyond the expanse of mangroves. The heat, quiet, stillness, and vastness somehow recall a desert region in the American Southwest, despite the mud and lush vegetation surrounding you. Crabs and mudskippers pop out of the sandy-gray dirt and plunge back into their holes; white water birds swoop down onto the wetlands to peck around, or take a slow walk with you. When the boardwalk ends, you keep walking, past yellow paper lanterns hanging around a dilapidated house, past bikers taking a rest who will later overtake you, and past Buddhas lined up against a brick building. Then you reach Tamsui, the town along an estuary that leads to the Taiwan Strait. You gasp at pink plumeria flowers quivering in the salty breeze from the river — and at the shards of sunlight over the stretch of water. You have seen this view before. By the East River in New York, the Ala Wai Canal in Honolulu, the Seine in Paris, the Thames in London, and the Sumida in Tokyo. You sit on a bench to watch the glitter dance the way it does around the world, and stay until the sun drives you into the shade and then to the metro station.

Next morning, while waiting for your bus to the airport at the terminal, you go to a stall for breakfast and point at mysterious food items sorted in stainless containers. This, this, and that, you indicate to the woman who cuts up the food with scissors, tosses the pieces into a strainer, dips them in broth, and pours them into a plastic bag with spice and chopped scallions. You only recognize an egg; the others may be fish paste, or meat. You are never sure, and you like that, because you like this experience of eating unidentifiable street food from a plastic bag with chopsticks at a bus terminal.

Back in Tokyo. Given the short flight time and the city's East Asian atmosphere, you don't feel like you've returned from overseas. Yet you do feel different, just as you did after navigating through streets in North America and Europe. Now you know that any journeys to foreign destinations, nearby or faraway, lead you to equally spectacular views of the world.

# 8. Slow Down in the City

**Lindsay Gacad**

*June 2017, Upper West Side, NYC*

In the two avenues you have to cross to get from my apartment to my place of work, you pass three food trucks. The first one, on the corner of 66th and Broadway, in front of the Raymour and Flanigan furniture store, serves the best breakfast sandwiches and iced coffee. Two scrambled eggs, a sausage patty and a slice of yellow American cheese sizzling hot with some Cholula hot sauce or ketchup, seasoned with salt and pepper smashed between a sliced Kaiser roll. Sometimes you'd get a whiff of cumin or adobo spice, so you ask her, finally realizing there was a whole menu pasted on the side of the truck, do you make tamales? As she fills your large plastic to-go cup with the dark amber iced coffee, she tells you yes and the best one is chicken. This disappoints you a bit. You never want chicken, pork is always the way to go, then beef, maybe even fish too, then chicken is last, as you find it is often dried out or bland. At the same time, someone else in a suit has come up to get his bagel and orange juice; another woman picks up a hot coffee; they're all exchanging bills, coins and quarters with her. She slides her hands from the counter giving them change effortlessly, blank-faced. And because you want to please her, you order one chicken and one beef tamale. And because she is proud of her product, she shrugs and says, "Okay," looking passé, but nodding because she is glad you have finally indulged. The tamales are steaming and small, wrapped in foil, the thinner kind that is mass produced in those purple boxes you see from all the street vendors. She gives you the bag and you're off to work at nine on the dot.

Next on the block between Broadway and Columbus Avenues, still on 66th St. is the Casbah truck. You didn't know it was called the Casbah truck until you looked on Yelp so you could tell your friends, no, convince your friends that yes there is some good and relatively fresh street meat on the Upper West Side. The two guys that work the truck wear red polo shirts and small red caps. One has a handsome face and always looks sweaty. He's usually the one chopping up the meat and sizzling the peppers and onions. He rarely steps out, but when he does, you're surprised that he has a little round belly and that he's only about 5'7". When he's in the truck he seems like a tall, dark-eyed mysterious chef who concocts those delicious middle eastern recipes, but in the daylight, on the street corner, he's kind of an ordinary Joe, or rather, Mohammed. Their truck is one of the larger ones as it covered with a beige and brown mural – a vibrant swath of falafel, shawarma, pitas, and kebabs. This is the source of the real cumin smell that at such an early hour can be a little abrasive on the nose. As you and all your coworkers rush with your breakfasts to the behemoth buildings of Disney-ABC Television, which take up the entire block of 66th and 67th streets all the way east to Central Park West, the smell of garlicky meat, tahini and bulgur wheat are not necessarily a match for the senses. Everyone is newly pressed, newly showered, doused in cologne and/or perfume. But of course you have come to love it and the fact that they are there, trusty and reliable, scrappy and consistent. As you pass, they are already preparing for the lunch rush which starts as early as 11 and you and the friendly, less handsome one share a genial nod.

One surprising morning, much like any other Thursday let's say, the sidewalk gets crowded because a homeless couple is sprawled out and sleeping against the wide windows of the Century 21 store. You start walking in the street because the crowds take up most of the space, darting and dodging, and because you hate seeing your coworkers right before you even enter the building, then you have to walk together all the way up and it seems there's never any relief from the inane small talk you both feel obliged to make. But you stop short when you realize there is a circular heap of excrement sitting on the curb, five feet away from the Casbah truck. You don't quite step in it, but you instinctively back away, stupidly into the street, dangerously near to the slow-moving traffic. The midnight blue Mercedes honks in spurts of three. You fear the potential wafting wind or even a hint of how it might smell. It is a jarring image, because it is so large and brown like the emoji with googly eyes, and it is almost perfectly shaped by someone who swirls soft serve. So you keep on walking, because you think to yourself that maybe it had come from the new homeless couple that now live on your street and who on earth would have the awful job of cleaning up such a mess? Ill-equipped with a dustpan and broom?

The third and final truck is right outside the studio doors over where the now Kelly and Ryan show is, which used to be Regis and Kelly. This is a simple truck: they have cold pastries, cold bagels engorged with squares of plain full fat cream cheese, each served with two flimsy napkins. Their specialty is coffee, all kinds of flavors and special milks, dairy, non-dairy, soy, almond, hemp. The sweetness is what catches the wind here, the bear claws and cherry danishes meld with the turbinado natural brown sugar or caramel syrup that my colleagues drown in their joe. The guys that man this truck are white, maybe Polish? I cannot place the accent, but they're older gentlemen who remember your order and call you sweetheart or my love with a familiarity that's acceptable from two older gentlemen in a tin cart, confined to an arm's reach. You're grateful for them and their determination to remain unchanged. You imagine everything they've seen from this spot starting at 6am, greeting the guests and celebs that rush in to the show, serving them coffee just before they are camouflaged in wigs, makeup and studio lights.

# 9. A Moment of Truth in the Andes

**Steve Gardiner**

*Climbing Nevado Pisco*
*July 19, 1982*

I crept to the edge of the crevasse and looked down. It was a
narrow crack, only three feet across at the top, so I could see
down fifteen feet, then the curving sides created darkness and
mystery below. I glanced at the snow on the opposite side. Since
we were ascending, the other side was higher than where I stood.
I would have to jump both out and up. It was not far, but a little
awkward.

I took a few steps back, made sure there was some slack
in the rope, took three quick steps, and leaped across the
crevasse. I landed solidly on the crusted snow and moved on.
Ten feet later, I faced another crevasse. The slope we were on
was a jumble of ice blocks and crevasses, splitting the glacier in
every direction. I jumped across that crevasse and landed on a
flat, secure area. It was be a good place to stop, set up a belay,
and let Karl climb up to me.

"Karl, I'm safe on a good platform," I said. "Come on
up. The belay's on."

"Climbing," Karl said.

I watched him wind his way up the slope, jumping over
the same series of crevasses I had just jumped. He moved
smoothly, efficiently. I had just met Karl two days before in the
village of Huaraz in the Andes Mountains of Peru. We had agreed
to climb Nevado Pisco together, but our planning did not include
a route with this many crevasses. The conditions on the mountain
were not normal, and we had both expressed concern about the
broken nature of the glacier.

Karl climbed up to the flat area and stood beside me. He
took a couple deep breaths. We were at just over 17,000 feet

elevation, so the lack of oxygen was noticeable. After a brief pause, Karl continued upward, jumping over two more crevasses.

"The next crevasse is wider, but there is a snow bridge across it," Karl said. "It looks like I can walk across it."

Karl probed the bridge with his ice axe and moved slowly onto it. From my angle, it looked like the crevasse was six or seven feet wide. That meant he could probably see farther down inside the crack. While that doesn't necessarily make it more dangerous, it makes it appear more dangerous. He moved carefully, stepping gently onto the bridge. I let out just enough rope to allow him to move but tight enough to catch him quickly if the bridge collapsed. The bridge proved strong, and Karl walked across and continued winding his way through the crevasses. Some of the smaller ones he could walk around, others he jumped.

I had never been on a glacier fractured this badly. I had jumped crevasses and crossed snow bridges before, but never in such a concentrated mass. I watched Karl climbing ahead. He was from southern Germany and had several years of climbing experience in the Alps of Switzerland, France, and Italy. He had told me stories about his climbs there, and as I watched him climb, he seemed confident. I felt reassured.

He reached another flat spot and set a belay anchor. When he was ready, I moved upward and continued the process of jumping over the gaps and walking on the snow bridges. I felt the gentle tug of the rope as Karl belayed it, giving me good protection on the precarious slope.

When I reached Karl, we looked at the glacier above. More fractures. More problems. We had been climbing for three hours, breathing the thin air, and needed a break before we tackled the chaos above. I looked at one crevasse about fifty feet above us. It appeared wider, darker than the others, and the upper edge was three or four feet higher than the lower edge. It was my turn to lead, and I needed a few minutes to think about that before I would have the courage to attack that one.

My wife Peggy and I had arrived in Huaraz four days earlier. We had read about the village for months and had dreamed about traveling there. We wanted to visit the village and see the spectacular mountains of the Cordillera Blanca (the White Range) of the Andes Mountains that are just outside town.

We were working as teachers at Colegio Roosevelt, the American School in Lima. We had been living in Lima for four months, so we had grown accustomed to all the honking horns, screeching tires, and crowded streets and buses. In Huaraz, it was so quiet. That was what we noticed the most. We walked along the sidewalks, talked with the people, and enjoyed the bright sun. We knew the fog was heavy in Lima, but in Huaraz, Huascaran, the highest peak in Peru, dominated the skyline, completed the void in the end of the valley—the Callejon de Huaylas they call it—and gave us a spectacular view the Andes Mountains.

After two hours of walking through the streets and looking in the shops, my wife Peggy and I stopped by the Hotel Barcelona, the center of activity for climbers coming into the Huaraz area. We planned to ask around for information about the routes, snow and rock conditions, and the possibility of finding other partners to join us on a climb. Huaraz, like much of Peru and South America was having a bad year for tourists, and consequently, we found no one at the Barcelona interested in climbing. We learned nothing about the routes or climbing conditions. We did find one note in Spanish and English posted by a climber who was looking for partners to accompany him on Nevado Pisco, a peak which has become popular because of its prime location between the mountains of Huandoy and Huascaran. I left a note in response.

That evening he came to the Hotel Andino where we were staying to meet us. He introduced himself as Karl Ritsert. He said he was eager to try a climb in the Cordillera Blanca. None of us had climbed in the area before, and as always, there is a concern about climbing in unfamiliar terrain.

Literature and history are filled with the stories of humans facing the unknown, and even in our modern times, the feeling is no different. That hesitation produces the anticipation, the adrenaline, that changes the act of climbing from one of pure physical work to an experience of life.

Unfamiliarity was furthered in this case by the fact that Peggy and I had not climbed with Karl before. I would have preferred a partner that I knew and had developed a trust-relationship with, but that situation was not available. New mountains. A new partner. If we wanted to climb, we would have to take what we had and go. What did the Andes have in store for us?

Peggy had had a head cold for the previous two days. In the afternoon she was feeling very ill. In the evening, she seemed better, and we thought she would be fit for the climb.

The packs were ready.

So were we.

In the morning, we met Karl, got a bus from Huaraz to Yungay, the tiny village nearest the park entrance. The trailhead was at a series of lakes called Lagunas Llaganuco. To get there from Yungay, we would ride in the back of a truck. The driver told us he wanted to wait for enough people to fill the truck before he drove us to the lakes.

On the bus ride to Yungay, Karl, in his soft-spoken way, told us interesting stories of the two months he had just spent in Bolivia. We were lucky that his English was good, because our German was non-existent. His Spanish was also good. Intelligent and friendly he was a special find for us in a foreign country. Isn't it interesting that we come from mountainous areas, and we met so far from our respective homes because of a shared interest, a mutual passion for the mountains?

When the driver had enough passengers in his truck, he steered it toward the lakes. In the back of the truck, we had a great view of the peaks of the Cordillera Blanca. We climbed up the valley just to the left of Huascaran. Climbers are always dreamers, and we gazed at the magnificent peak. We imagined its ridges and couloirs. We envisioned the summit and its view. Maybe someday we would return to give that one a try.

The first half of the trip was all Huascaran, but after the park entrance, other snowy giants took their turn on stage, and we felt like small specks in an other-worldly environment. Green lakes. Vast meadows. Vertical rock. Jagged ice. Land of awe.

The driver took us directly to the trailhead. We unloaded our packs, ate a quick snack, and set out on a well-defined trail. At the end of the box canyon, the trail switchbacked up and exited to the left over a pass. Through there, we found a pampa with a house and a herd of cattle. These people were living at nearly 15,000 feet. That is higher than the tallest summit in the continental United States. It is a different life here.

Another five hundred feet of climbing brought us to the lake at the base of Pisco. All around the lake are the rocky deposits of ice-age glaciers. In the midst of these moraines, previous climbers have scooped out level tent sites. We took advantage of one of them. Karl had no tent, but used a bivouac bag just outside of our North Face dome tent. It had taken us four hours to hike to base camp. We arrived at six pm, set up camp, and cooked in the dark.

On the hike in, Peggy had to drop back. She wasn't feeling well at all, so I walked with her. Her cold persisted and had weakened her. We doubted if her cold would improve at 15,800 feet, so we discussed alternatives for approaching the climb. We decided to climb higher, set up the tent, and leave the gear with her there. Then Karl and I would try the glacier. Karl had walked fast on the trail to the lake. I wondered if I would be able to stay with him on the climb.

Climbing is often a big puzzle. It all makes sense when the pieces go together, but getting them in place is often extremely difficult.

We rose before sunrise, ate, and scrambled up a large boulder field to a massive bench, then up a river gully to a flat ledge just below the glacier at 16,500 feet elevation. That was a good place to pitch the tent. We made sure Peggy was comfortable and left her there with our extra gear. Karl and I headed for the summit.

We followed the top of a morainal ridge toward the glacier, hoping it would connect. It didn't. We had to drop and reclimb 300 feet and then climb 200 feet more to reach the glacier.

Karl led an incredible ice escarpment 35 feet high just to get onto the glacier. Twice his crampons lost purchase and grated against the rough ice. At last, from behind an ice wall, he belayed me securely, and I struggled up.

As I climbed, I saw patches of blood on the ice, and when I crested the ice ridge where Karl sat, I saw his hand. Ice as sharp as a knife had sliced the knuckles on all four fingers of his left hand. Blood was dripping into the snow at his feet. He bandaged the cuts. I gave him my extra pair of wool mittens, and we continued our climb.

Ahead of us was an astounding maze of broken glacial blocks, seracs, crevasses, and steep snow. We would climb a rope length, stop and discuss how to pass a crevasse or how to climb over or around a frozen obstacle. I had seen glaciers broken this badly before, but always from a safe distance. Ice falls cascaded down the mountain on both sides of us. Jagged chunks of ice, icicles, spires, and gaping crevasses were everywhere.

We jumped over the black holes, slowly crossed the snow bridges, waded through thigh-deep snow, and balanced on steep icy slopes. Many times we overcame one obstacle only to find another just behind it or around it. We climbed and turned and jumped and dropped and climbed some more. Every step brought new angles of beauty—new perspectives of the alien world we were discovering.

If the glacier wasn't pretty enough, all we had to do was look in any direction. Below us were the glacier, the curved spine of the moraine, the yellow tent where Peggy waited, and the crystal blue lake in the valley, curving to the right and west toward Yungay. Straight ahead was the summit of Pisco. To the left were the four summits of the Huandoy massif. To the right was the impossibly severe Chacraraju. Behind us were the double summits of Huascaran and the symmetrical wonder of Chopicalqui. Any one of those peaks alone was beauty defined in concrete form. Together they were overwhelming.

We found it harder to breathe. I had only been at this altitude once before, and for Karl this was his highest. After half a day of climbing, we were no longer fresh. Even though this was exactly what we wanted, why we had come here, rest stops became more frequent.

At 18,000 feet, we paused, and I thought about the bigger crevasse above, wondering if I would be able to find a way over or around it. By then, our water supply was low, so Karl readied his stove to melt snow. He filled the pot, and we ate while the snow sizzled.

After ten minutes, the pot was filled with water. We decided to give it another couple of minutes to get hotter. The stove tipped. Water splattered on the food sack and instantly disappeared into the snow. We looked at each other, knowing that precious water had been lost and precious time wasted.

Karl tried to re-light the stove. It wouldn't. He opened the fuel cap. No gasoline. The extra bottle was in his pack in the tent with Peggy. No water. Not enough time. A biting cold wind reminded us too vividly of the hot water we almost had. No choice. We had to retreat.

I looked up at the black crevasse above. I would never know if I could lead it or not. We took as many pictures of the ice, the rock, and the panorama as our fingers could stand, quickly repacked our gear, and plunge-stepped down the tracks we had made on the ascent.

Backing off a climb is not easy. Time, energy, and emotion are invested in an attempt to combine a good experience with the chance to stand on a summit. We did not reach the top that day, but we had both received an introduction to the Andes and had a memorable experience. It would be impossible to feel regret about a peak which had given us so much.

Our descent was a happy one, though not carefree. We belayed the snowbridges and crevasse-jumpings as we had done going up. Many climbing accidents happen on the downclimb when a party has relaxed assuming the climb is over. We would not, and did not, make that mistake.

On the steep descent off the foot of the glacier, Karl thought enough to leave one of his axes placed with a carabiner attached to provide one point of protection for me. A kind and intelligent gesture.

We followed the moraine back to where Peggy sat in the sun reading a book and waiting for us. We packed the tent and gear, and hiked down to the base camp lake. We rejoined the nicely-constructed trail, walked down to the large pampa which proved too wet for camping, and finally pitched the tent next to a stream at the base of the switchbacks in the box canyon. From the three sides of this box, five separate multi-level waterfalls tumbled into the valley. Their roar and the increased density of oxygen provided our little-needed sleeping tablets for the night.

In the morning, we reached the lakes in an hour where we received terrible news. We talked with a French party that spent the night in the stone shelters at the lakes. One of their members, a woman, died of heart trouble during the night, and her body was inside the shelter. They had contacted the authorities at the park entrance station and were waiting for someone to investigate before they could remove the body. They would have to wait, maybe for hours, for the authorities to arrive. I shuddered to think of all the difficulties they would have, the language barrier, the paperwork, the transportation problems, all stacked on top of the emotional burden of losing a friend. They had come to the lakes for the natural beauty, enjoyment, and confrontation of the unknown — just as we had — and they had paid a tremendous price for it.

Two of them entered the shelter and returned, tears in their eyes. I couldn't look at them. Our experience had been good and contrasted so dramatically with theirs. Another chapter in our introduction to the Andes.

In camp the night before, Karl, Peggy, and I had talked about climbing in the Alps and about climbing in the States and how different it is from the Cordillera Blanca. The dimensions in the Andes are beyond any imaginings we had in our home climbing grounds, and with that increase in dimensions comes an increase in challenge, an increase in meeting that challenge, and a disproportionate increase in the dangers involved in the sport. The Andes appear as a world set apart, a world of their own, with a different set of rules and codes. They are immense, powerful, beautiful, and dangerous.

My curiosity about the peaks of the Cordillera Blanca had been justified. They are worth every bit of consideration a climber can give them. Our first Andean climb had been all we wanted. It provided us with a varied experience, a new friend, and a close look at a different place and lifestyle. What more could we ask for?

Waiting for the truck back to Yungay, we talked about the glacier on Nevado Pisco. Crossing the snow bridges and jumping the crevasses had pushed me into a new realm, and the images in my mind were powerful.

"I just want to thank you," I said to Karl. "When we were up there in the middle of that jumbled ice, I was pretty nervous. I had never seen anything like that. Knowing about your experience in the Alps and watching you climb made me feel confident that we were OK."

Karl turned to look at me. "Really? That's not right. I have never climbed in conditions that difficult. I knew you had climbed in the Tetons and on Mt. Rainier and that made me believe you were comfortable with what we were doing. That's why I stayed with the climb as long as I did. It seems we created a sense of security for each other."

# 10. Over the Edge and Back

**Daniel Gabriel**

*The West, USA*

Back in the day, hitchhiking was my steadiest form of transport. It took me across dozens of countries over the years, but this jaunt from March 1970 has always stuck with me. It was a mid-winter hitch of epic distance that was nearly my last.

What kicked it off was Spring Break — and a burning desire for the comparative warmth and freak frenzy of San Francisco. I was a nineteen-year-old college sophomore who had just spent a near eternity — or at least four months — suffering under the icy lash of a Minnesota winter. The fact that I was 2000 miles away from the West Coast and had only $30 to my name was no deterrent.

In fact, things started off quite well. Heading west with my travel partner Randall went so smoothly that we outpaced the Greyhound, the Union Pacific, and even the standard optimal driving time. A mere fifty hours after setting out we were walking up to our buddies Hal and Walt's place in Berkeley. In eastern Nebraska we had picked up my longest ride ever — 1600 miles — with a guy who drove his Charger so long and so fast that even car troubles in Salt Lake City didn't hold us up unduly.

We spent four warp-speed days in the West, with the lines of sleeping bags on Hal and Walt's floor ebbing and flowing as chance, circumstance, and the vagaries of love dictated sleeping arrangements. If our hike up Mt. Tamalpais was an obvious high, the run-in with two flashback-addled Vietnam vets in the Haight was a sobering reminder that not all casualties are declared on the battlefield. Still, between the fast break hitch west and our goofball pick-up basketball games enlivened by plates of special brownies, I had this trip nailed and pegged as a roaring success.

Coming back was something else altogether. Six of us set off in a "driveaway" — a car being transferred from one city to another, with us volunteering as drivers — the morning after an all-night acid test. As the only non-participant in the hallucinogenic melee, it fell to me to organize the departure. This won me no friends and a long, headachy morning at the wheel scooting through Bay Area rush hour traffic.

The six of us had arrived out West almost simultaneously, as part of a grand neo-Prankster scheme. We'd hitched out in three duos. One set had ridden freight trains most of the way, freezing over the Rockies in unheated cars. The second set had been hampered by one member's uncertainty — Big Dave (it sometimes seemed that half my friends were named Dave and, indeed, three of the six in our car were) had been scheduled to be inducted into the Army and his road west led him ever further away, and ever closer to a possible jail term for dodging the draft. Between rides he would occasionally jump back onto the other side of the road and frantically begin hitching back towards Minneapolis and his waiting draft board.

Now, on our return journey, he'd already missed his induction date and found himself in the somewhat contrary position of returning to the scene of the crime. Had he known he would end up doing six months in a St. Louis prison he might never have come along.

The first day out wasn't too bad, despite the lack of legroom and food money. But as we cruised up into the high plateau of southern Wyoming, rumbling through the Rockies, we hit a snowstorm. A bad one. Bad enough to drive most all other traffic off the road. We had no such margin for delay. The driveaway was due in Chicago and I needed to be showing my face on the first day of spring quarter classes at the University of Minnesota. Failure to appear when attendance was taken on opening day meant one forfeited the spot in the class and I certainly couldn't risk blowing an entire term's work, especially since tuition would not be refunded.

We rode the lonesome highways through Wyoming cowboy country all through the night, staying on the blacktop by sticking to 25-30 mph. When nobody else could see to drive, Big

Dave offered. I was in the front seat, riding shotgun. "No faster than 30," I said. "It's way too slick."

"What do you think I am?" he said, but I let the opportunity pass.

Everybody but he and I went to sleep, so that I was the only one who saw him edge the car up to 35 and before I could even attempt to issue a caution, there was a soft little nudge from somewhere and we were sliding sideways down the interstate, across our two lanes, over the bare median, across the far two lanes with a semi blaring its horn as it bore down upon us, and then we were over the roadside edge into pitch darkness, hurtling down a thirty foot embankment with the rest of the guys coming awake in fits and starts.

Straight down the snow-glittering embankment (oh shit, what happened to the sky?), out across the fields (thump, bump, which ones are rocks? What if — thump) to smack to a stop (huh — wham — what?) on a ridge of snow. Above us in the dark the semi had shuddered to a halt. A figure emerged, running, with a beam of light. Behind him, more semis began to stop.

We ran the gamut of terror, relief, confusion . . . and settled on disgust at Big Dave for trying to hurry us into our graves.

An hour later we'd pushed the car through the snow to a more level section of verge where we could fire it up — amazingly, it still ran — and blitz our way back onto the interstate. Big Dave was strapped into the back seat and told to stay quiet. I grabbed the wheel and marched us east towards dawn. In the early morning the snow lightened and we pulled into the last rest stop in Wyoming for gas and as much food as we could muster between us. The cowboys in the cafe looked none too pleased to see us (Couldn't have been the War Moratorium arm bands, could it?), but the two frantic hitchhikers huddled outside wrapped in their sleeping bags went down on their knees to plead for a ride. With six of us already aboard, we had absolutely nowhere to put them. "We don't dare even wait inside," they said; that, we could understand.

We packed them in, with one lying across the feet of the guys in back and the other squeezed like a soft banana into the well of the rear window. Now we were eight, with almost no visibility, and still a need to keep moving east.

Big Dave pleaded to be allowed another chance. It was daylight, and the storm had stopped. Surely the worst was over. Like a parent giving in to a whiny child, we let him . . .

Less than an hour later, with the border practically in sight, we came over a bridge, again going just a bit too fast (though my protests had been shouted down by the others as "fascist"), hit a patch of ice on the downward side and shot like lightning off the road. This time we weren't so lucky as to hit a snow drift. It was straight into a tree.

Bam! My nose hit the windshield, shattering my glass sunglasses and leaving a quick, severe headache in its wake. The front of the car was caved in like a vee, and water was shooting from the radiator. Around me, bodies were piling out of the car — "Look out! It might explode!" — and we tumbled into the snow yet again.

My nose and a spot above my eye were bleeding onto my coat and Tom, who'd been squeezed next to a window in the back, was swinging his right arm and swearing like a sailor. Randall kept saying, "Do you hear that ringing? What's that ringing?" — but I spun him towards the trunk and we started passing out our gear.

Once we'd grabbed our packs, we all turned to berate Big Dave. But he'd taken off running the minute the car hit and was even now flagging down a semi, pointing to us and climbing aboard. Gone for help? Or just disappearing? No telling, but all the rest of us knew we had better do something similar. This driveaway had been put in the care of just two guys; all the rest of us were extra baggage that could mean some severe penalties if found. We divvied up hitching spots and took off in several directions. My odds on making those first day classes were not looking good.

Randall and I eventually flagged a ride of our own and no sooner had we started telling our woeful story to the two college-age guys who'd stopped than we came around a bend in the Nebraska interstate to see two sleeping bags standing upright on the roadside with thumbs waggling out the tops.

It was against road etiquette, but I had to do it: "Please," I said to the driver. "Stop for these guys. They were with us."

He did, and now once again there were six of us barreling down the highway jabbering about the day's events. Eventually the adrenaline rush wore off and we napped in contorted positions. I woke as the car pulled off the road (any sudden change in direction had me spooked by now) and into a gas station. After we'd filled, the driver asked me "How much is it?" — which seemed odd as the pump showing the price was right next to his window. Then when we needed to pull back onto the road, it took his pal in the shotgun seat to show him where the on-ramp was.

We found out the score later, when the first driver finally traded seats and napped. His buddy told us, "He's legally blind. Can't hardly see a thing. No problem as long as the road is straight . . ."

I was the only one heading north, so they dropped me outside of Des Moines in the gathering dusk and the car rolled further east. I tramped a couple of cloverleafs that seemed to go nowhere useful and finally found my way north to Minnesota. I hadn't realized how I looked until I got picked up by a kindly gent heading home to his farm in southern Minnie and he gaped as I got in. I spun my tale and then, when I should have been perky and companionable, felt my head drop onto my shoulders. He'd told me he was going just over the border and three different times he woke me, saying his turn-off was coming up. Each time I fell back asleep before he could get there and the good-hearted fellow kept on driving north. He finally dropped me at an empty Greyhound station and promised that a bus would be coming on through. It was 9 a.m. when I hit town, blood splattered down my shirt and jacket, glass from my sunglasses embedded on my collar, starving, wild-eyed and tired beyond all imagining.

But I made my classes.

Six weeks later Tricky-Dick Nixon announced the expansion of the Indochina War into Cambodia, and a nationwide student strike shut campuses down across the country. Spring term was over.

# 11. My Name Is Mai

**JL Hall**

*Bangkok*

Every time I climb the stairs to the Skywalk, I look for her. For Mai, small and filthy in her yellow dress. She sits here against a pillar, baht scattered and glinting around her, a tattered cardboard sign propped in her lap etched in marker pen that says: My Name Is Mai.

I think she is three or four, tiny for her age. Her fingers and soles are dark with the ingrained dirt of a beggar. Her dress is full of Bangkok's dust and stink, its edges are blackened, as are the gold bracelets on her wrists and ankles. The diamond earrings that stud her ears are dulled. Here, in the broiling heat, suspended between the heavens and the thunder of the traffic below, she sits motionless and mute. Her eyes are dead.

Every time I climb the stairs I crane my neck to see who has left her. Are they here, watching? Is there a gang or only a pimp? She is dark skinned; has she been trafficked from the rural north, Cambodia, or Myanmar? How long before I arrived did they deposit her, seat her against the pillar and steal away, creeping down the stairs to melt into the throng and leave this toddler, whom I have never seen move or speak, alone without protection.

I come every day along the Skywalk. I tell myself that this is the best route from the city to National Stadium station where I return home to my guesthouse. My palm is hot with the baht that I clutch in it, in the evenings my fingers smell of brass. I drop the coins in front of Mai, resisting the urge to crouch and touch her, to pull her to me, to scoop her into my arms and to run, to speed her away from this fucking existence, this fate worse than death. Instead, I hover, I drop my change with a tinkle onto the concrete, and pause, waiting for her to glance up. To connect, to give her human warmth. To show her love. But she never does.

Sometimes I leave water and titbits of food, but I worry that it is worse for her, that she might be punished.

The Skywalk heaves with shoppers and commuters, school children and backpackers. Women clasping pastel-coloured plastic bags of market vegetables. Office workers eating moo ping from the hawkers in the street below and whose aroma coils up above the traffic fumes. If you stop for a moment you feel the vibration: the footfall, the traffic, and at points the roar of the Skytrain overhead as it hurdles from station to station. The floor shakes, just slightly, but constantly. In the middle of this maelstrom sits Mai, small and unseen.

It is now May. Bangkok is febrile with political protests and bloodshed. The sky is stained yellow from tear gas and black from smoke: the city burns in the streets where the battles between red-shirts and the army are fought. The heat builds, mercury rising with the conflict, and now the surreal mania of Songkran, Thailand's New Year and water festival. Amid the terror, Thai teenagers fire day-glo water pistols at one another and drench pedestrians with buckets of water for sanuk, for fun.

One day I pass along the Skywalk with coins pressed in my hand to find that Mai is not here. I halt, confused, before retracing my steps: I must have passed her, perhaps she was hidden by the crowd. Perhaps I haven't reached her yet, perhaps she has been moved. I pace back and forth between Chit Lom and National Stadium stations: she is gone. So I wait. I loiter, toeing my flip-flops on the concrete, my back slick with sweat as I lean on the railing. Mai doesn't appear. I begin to wonder if I am being watched, if her pimp won't leave her here; maybe I have been spotted before. Perhaps, like other do-gooding Westerners before me, there is a risk I might interfere, or pointlessly call the police. After a while I give up and return home in the fading light to my guesthouse where I think about her as I lie in bed and wonder where she sleeps, if she has a bed, if she has food, if she has anyone who is ever kind to her. If in her wretched life she is ever, ever safe.

I don't see Mai again. I leave for London not long after this; Bangkok is increasingly violent, and news reports of murdered journalists and injured civilians are reaching concerned family and friends in Britain. There are rumours of impending airport occupations and road blockages. I flee the country like all travellers eventually do: impotent, guilty, and ultimately selfish.

I think of Mai today, some ten years later as I sit with a student in her final tutorial and notice the smallness of her hands, they are almost miniature. I stare at them as she is talking and gesticulating, asking me questions that I no longer hear. Mai will be a teenager now, if she has lived. She will have been prostituted and raped and perhaps sold and trafficked out of Thailand. Perhaps she has ended up in prison, with her veins full of needle-sticks and heroin. If she is lucky, she will be painted and gaudy in the neon sois of Patpong with the other bar-girls and pimps where she retreats up dingy stairs to be groped and penetrated by Westerners whose baht lie scattered and glinting around her. This would be a fate better than a fate worse than death.

My student is from Thailand, from a wealthy family. She will shortly return there to work in her parents' jewelry business and study gemology. She tucks a strand of hair behind her ear and her diamond studs glitter. She wishes me well and thanks me for her help, for the difference I made.

"I did nothing," I say.

# 12. Make Believe

### Rebecca Hart Olander

We made a temporary home just up the hill from the Colosseum,
walked the dusty track of ancient chariots, ate as if our lives depended on it,
all manner of pasta with clams, beef, bacon, and lobster, Chianti from a basket-
bottomed bottle, and water, still, or gassed, from vessels of tall green glass.

We made coffee in a silver device screwed together at the center,
only room for one at a time, and sat drinking it looking out across rooftops
over edifices tinged terracotta and sunflower, the shade of the paintings
still gracing the tomb walls within the catacombs of San Sebastian.

We made a nuclear quartet again, the pieces of our family puzzle
joining as we walked labyrinthine streets in search of sights
we'd seen by day but hoped to see again at night, dogged by exhaustion
and the ever-present exhaust from the tailpipes of scooters and tiny cars.

We made good time on foot, crossing to the seedy side of Rome
where street vendors sold coiled scarves with the same ten patterns,

red with white polka dots, paisley blue, repeating table after
table, as if
to break us down incrementally, to make us say Enough already,
I'll take one.

We made reservations without plans, open to seeing what we'd
see,
but then, amidst the ruinous present, couldn't help but study
the map,
searching for how it could take us to the Mouth of Truth, or the
secret keyhole
of the Knights of Malta beside Santa Sabina church atop the
Aventine Hill.

We made tourist mistakes, trying to wave a bus down but only
managing to bid
the driver buongiorno, then hopping on the wrong bus as it
hurtled past the pyramid
beside the Protestant cemetery we'd been aiming for, so that we
had to disembark
and take a subway back to where we'd missed Keats and
Shelley's bones.

Three out of four of us took a plane home, but we left our
oldest child by the gate
to make her way to another country as we crossed through
secure borders
and spent the last of our brightly colored bills on lemon-tinged
olive oil and wine.

We'd made it seem as if she hadn't grown up and away, as if we
had the right
to chide about bedtimes and packing. We even made believe
that we were just
on holiday, not running from future ghosts, and all those
broken urns and columns

of curling travertine leaves let us think we were right, that the past can be
recovered from. That slaves didn't turn every cog and push every oxen,
that good fences make good neighbors, that we'd come back again someday,

would stand again under domed ceilings painted with stars, would even be able
to preserve what we have right now. A pretense that every day isn't like being
raised on a wooden elevator into a cheering throng who hope to see you bleed.

## How, Drinking One Monday in Massachusetts, I Remembered What I Felt
## on the Carrer de Mallorca in Spain One Long-Ago Winter

The nickel-sized portal at the mouth of a bottle of beer
provides passage into another world, triggering spirit,
and in the time it takes for fruit to reach perfection without
tipping into overripe, the space between the trip and the fall,

I'm back in Barcelona, where Gaudi's
architecture was an undoing in its doing,
the way the hands of someone desired can
untie deep knots you didn't know were there.

As I stood looking up at the Basílica de la Sagrada Família,
the bag of oranges in my fist the only thing tethering me
to my friend (we had said we'd share them, and it was my turn
to swing the netted sack as we walked along), questions fell away.

Later, on the train to Toledo, the feeling of faith followed
me, as if it were there to stay. I don't know when
it left, but what saddens me most is that I didn't
immediately notice that it was gone.

Oh, Awe, oh God, why can't you be undeniable, like gravity?
Why must your constancy be like my old flower press,
its screws rusted wings, and inside, after a season, the same
brown dust, smaller, and duller, than before?

# 13. Grapetree Bay, Saint Croix, Afternoon

**Greg Hill**

Three terns perch on the breaker.
Like the pelicans this morning,
they face the trade wind, but now the sun behind them
helps dry their little white feathers.

The pelicans have moved
down to the rocks that have soaked in the heat of the day.
From their crags and perches, they will watch the tide     tumble
below them. When the sun sinks lower, the pelicans will unfurl
into pillars of warm air to search
for fresh school fish.
But for now, each end of the beach is the dominion of content
birds.
The tide keeps washing in, keeps crashing against the rocks,
keeps time.
The afternoon is too hot for flying and diving. Even the
sunburnt beachgoers
relish the warm, slow hours to nap before mango daiquiris and
evening.

# 14. Spilled Blood

**Robert Kunizinger**

*Russia*

Dear Dad,

It's our first day out on the Trans-Siberian rail and we share a cabin with two young, Russian businessmen. I haven't picked up much of their conversation yet, but they are either finishing work in Petersburg and headed home, or they live in the city and are on their way to a job. My language skills are weak at best and communication is poor. It is so poor, in fact, that no one here knows we speak English; they think it is Spanish. When we tell them it's English they assume we are from England, and I let them for now. If I can break through to deeper conversation with anyone perhaps then I'll give them more details of where we're from and where we're going.

It seems no one we've met travels very far on the Siberian railroad. A few stops mostly in third class, or if they are in a cabin, one or two nights and certainly not all the way to Vladivostok. When we first boarded, the conductor asked where our final destination was and I said "Vladivostok" to which he recoiled. This isn't a tourist route; for that people head south to Moscow and cross Russia into Mongolia and China, ending up in Beijing. Besides, St Petersburg to Vladivostok is roughly the same distance by train as traveling from New York to Guam. We are an anomaly.

We started heading east out of St. Petersburg and will travel roughly three weeks with stops and wandering, but the first leg to Yekaterinburg is about two days. We opted for the north route to the city, which used to be the playground of the Czars. Of course, it was just one hundred years ago Nicholas the Second and his son Alexi took this train on this route to that city for what would be the last ride of their lives. I suppose the train is accustomed to fathers and sons. It appears to be a "man's" journey as I have seen very few women on board except for an attendant in each car and several in the dining car. When Nicholas and Alexei rode this rail from St. Petersburg to Yekaterinburg, they didn't fare so well. They, along with Alexandra and her four daughters, including Anastasia, were all slaughtered in the basement of a palace at our next stop. It is a shrine now. Tomorrow we will visit.

This is nothing like the Long Island Rail Road, Dad. How many years did you ride that from the outreaches of Suffolk County to Wall Street? I remember going with you when the five of us went to the city for dinner. We made it to midtown and I wanted to light a candle at St. Patrick's Cathedral. You were tired, and it was out of our way, but we went. It is odd how the Siberian rail feels safer and less shaky. Still I wish you were here. That was so long ago, wasn't it? I would love to ride trains with you again, talk about baseball, and have a drink in the bar car; you'd read the paper and I'd look out the window until we went underground. If you were here you'd order the burger and fries and have a Baltika 7, their best beer, and of course we would have some caviar just to be able to go back home and say we had caviar.

Funny how you just never know when the last ride will be. I wonder if Nicholas looked out at the same birch forests I'm staring at and had some sort of premonition akin to the doom Rasputin warned him about, his own family's death, the fall of his empire. Did his son stand nearby like Michael stands near me now? Did his young heart still hold hope that the hard days were past, and they'd now settle into some routine far from the war-torn city they always knew as home? Did he smile and think with simplicity about being able to spend more time with his parents? He was with his Dad for God's sake; what could possibly go wrong? When I was young, and we traveled to the city, I always felt safe and knew that somehow you'd figure it out. I assume Alexei felt the same around his exiled father. I suppose Michael too, waits for my cue to disembark, to head to the dining car, to settle in for the night. I've come to understand finally that you were as nervous as I am, wanting your son to have the time of his life yet protect him in a world of strangers.

It helps to imagine our two strange young Russian cabin mates are as apprehensive as us, wondering who these two Spaniards or Englishmen (or whoever the hell we are to them) are. Well at the least we have each other to secure our comfort zone. Traveling alone would be the true adventure. But I wasn't raised that way, was I? Safety first. Funny how many times I ignored that rule. Now, here I am hoping Michael wanders away, meets people and manages conversation. He'll play his harmonica; people will listen. He'll bring his chess set to the dining car and people will want to play. Music and chess are universal. Communication is easy; only language is burdensome.

Tomorrow we will be at the Church of the Spilled Blood, one of two Cathedrals with that moniker in this vast nation. Last week we went to the one where Alexander II was assassinated in St. Petersburg. Tomorrow we will see this one, built on the spot where his grandson, Czar Nicholas II, his wife Alexandra, his son Alexei, and the boy's four sisters were shot to death in the middle of the night. I'll light a candle for you.

*Always,*
　　*Robert*

# 15. The Reverse Florentine Gaze

**Wendy Kozma**

*Florence, Italy*

Florence overwhelmed me. Nestled in the heart of Italy, she was at once a loud, dominant presence with her constant flow of traffic, yet she was mysteriously relaxed. To the untrained visitor, she suggested that Florentines were in a mad rush to reach their destinations; motorcycles and bicycles weaved in and out of the labyrinth of traffic and were nudged by taxi drivers to get out of their way. Traffic was a constant moving pattern that frightened visitors but failed to unnerve the locals. Because to them, it suggested a hurried ease. It was this feeling, this graciousness, I hoped to acquire.

But weeks later, surrounded by a mixture of lush vegetation, fellow neighbors, and the dry rattle of Vespas, I worried that the feeling would leave the moment I left.

I sighed. It was almost riposo — time to close, shut down, reboot. Time to sleep. I found myself enjoying this lifestyle, perhaps too much, because only too soon would I find myself back in America, overcome with deadlines, appointments, and moving at a pace too fast. My real life. Part of me believed that life would be so much more relaxed, happier if I wasn't stressed about time. Yet, there was no escape from the perpetual, never ending tick-tock, tick-tock.

The tension that had left me slowly found its way back into my shoulders and made me grimace, and the sound of the clock became even louder in my mind. Things to do. Time to go. Now, now, now.

The cobblestone pavement and often narrow sidewalks of Florence made for both an interesting and harrowing journey, especially for someone like me who had a fear of falling. I worried that I would fall into oncoming traffic too and be stared at by passersby — a woman two sizes too large, unable to walk without stumbling, without grace and ease, but drivers tended to stop for pedestrians, tended to wait for them despite the perceived impatience to move. Eventually, I fell into the Florentine rhythm and didn't experience that worry as much — the staring, though, the watching me, well, that continued to bother me. When the sidewalks became too narrow or too crowded with people, I confidently stepped into the streets, walking down the middle of them without hesitation but conscious of being looked at.

From my apartment, I walked to the Duomo, the heart of Florence; it was what I sought when I became lost or confused on the many one way streets. The Duomo was the compass to move through the city. Not only did it aid in navigation, it was one of the most impressive cathedrals Italy had to offer. It spoke to Florentines and visitors alike — whispering a tale of magnificence, beauty, and history. But the locals walked or rode past the Duomo as though it was just another place, without seeming impressed. Its once copper façade now faded to green.

I came to Florence to enjoy its cathedrals and museums and the many shops and restaurants that lined the streets. The Duomo was just the beginning. I wanted to stop, to take in my surroundings. That was what I was supposed to do. Although I felt the need to see everything I could, I needed to slow down to truly appreciate the experience.

Time passed; people came and went; circumstances changed; events unfolded, enveloped me, and sometimes made me part of them. And I left traces that whispered I was there — in this world, that I was part of something extraordinary. That I was extraordinary.

Fascinated by the gods and goddesses in Greek & Roman mythology since I was a child, I was taken in by Botticelli's "The Birth of Venus" like so many before me. Beautiful, lithe, and born from sea foam. Her only purpose, her mission it would seem, to be a harbinger of love. And like Botticelli, I found Venus mysterious and alluring as she perched precariously on a seashell brought forth from the sea. The subtle look on the goddess's face suggested she was one who knew the strength of her own beauty; she was woman, goddess. All knowing. All powerful. Certain in purpose. It was a song she sang in that smile, small enough on her lips to be timid but sure enough to be knowing. She was mystery.

Until I found myself at the Uffizi Gallery in Florence, I had never gazed upon Botticelli's original. His mark was there — in the strokes of his brush, in the brilliant shades of pink and green. Beauty brought forth in those vibrant colors that swirled together on canvas to create seafoam and the gossamer shroud to cover Venus.

And when I finally encountered that mystery, I was overcome. Tears came unbidden, and for a moment, I wondered what other tourists must think of me as they rushed past — a grown woman standing in front of Botticelli's work, overwrought and crying. It was the details, the story that interested me as well as the work itself. And perhaps this work spoke to me because mythology helped shape my love of literature when I was a child, and besides, I had a story to tell myself.

I relished that time with the Botticelli and ignored those around me, hustling and bustling to get to the next room, the next famous painting. I embraced the beauty and the subtle use of lines and color, took my time, absorbed every line and curve, and committed it to memory.

I was seated at the Gusto Leo Ristorante on Via del Proconsolo the first time I had dinner by myself there. This was also the first time I felt completely confident in knowing where I was in Florence and comfortable enough to dine alone.

At the Gusto Leo, the waitress seated me at a table for two, so I deliberately chose to put my back towards the door, something I never did. The restaurant was what I would call a typical, run of the mill bar and grill, similar to what the States offer. The waitress gave me a menu and disappeared. She waited behind the counter until I motioned her over to either answer my questions or take my order. It occurred to me that I hadn't brought my usual protective gear, a book or writing material, when I went to a restaurant alone. I didn't even take out my cell phone. Usually, I felt out of place, awkward and preferred having something to do besides staring at my plate or at the empty seat opposite me. Instead, I leaned back in the chair, breathed deeply, and observed what was happening around me.

I ate slowly; I savored the richness of the gnocchi alla leo, and I knew that my waitress wouldn't acknowledge me again until I signaled, until I asked her for something else. She was not like American food servers; she didn't hover or bring me a second drink before I finished the first. She didn't bring me the bill before she offered me dessert. Instead, she took it for granted that I would stay until I was ready to leave, and I took it for granted that she wouldn't care when I did. She seemed disappointed that I didn't finish my gnocchi, that I asked for the check instead of dessert, but she gave it to me and then waited patiently for me to pay. I could have stayed at the Gusto Leo as long as I wanted; it wouldn't have mattered. What mattered to them was that I enjoyed my meal and that I would return.

Sitting outside the Duomo, I watched as the painter moved towards me. He sat up his small stand just in front of me where he spent every day, painting and selling his work; we made eye contact every day that I sat on the bench. Today, we nodded to one other, and I found my own thoughts amidst the noise and people.

At times, I felt self-conscious while I sat there. Most of the tourists and Florentines ignored me, but on more than one occasion, I cringed as people stopped to stare at me. Sometimes they pointed, and at least twice, they took pictures. I liked to think that they were taking photographs of something behind me or that they were gesturing to a statue or graffiti just beyond the bench, but I believe it was me that fascinated or horrified them. Had they never seen a woman my size before? Perhaps I was an anomaly to them, something that didn't register. Maybe it was because I was so beautiful that they stopped and stared, but I don't really believe that.

Sometimes, I engaged other English speakers in conversation. Because I couldn't readily understand the native language, sometimes I felt lonely when I sat there by myself for long periods of time. This was perhaps the most difficult part of my journey — not being able to speak the language, so I learned through experience. I spoke slowly, enunciated, and used a lot of hand gestures.

Despite the occasional tourist who stopped to stare, I reminded myself to stop, to breathe, to embrace what was in front of me. As I sat on my bench outside the Duomo in the heart of Florence, I watched the people; it was what I liked to do most when I traveled. I made up stories about them and tried my best not to stare at them the way I had been stared at. I gazed at one and then another and then shifted my attention, observing but conscious about being considered rude. I was encountering many people from many different places.

The tourists mingled with Florentines, eating gelato or buying goods from the many vendors who set up their wares every day, all day. Minimal traffic moved along the stretch of road before the Duomo; horse drawn carriages, bicycles, the occasional Vespa, emergency or police vehicles, and the random taxi weaved among the pedestrians who struggled to take that perfect picture. It was a loud place, teeming with multiple languages, wailing sirens, and the blowing wind.

The Duomo reminded me that I was in a city much older than the US and that I should relish the magnificence of its architecture and people. So I sat back on my bench and watched. I relaxed. I stretched, shifted positions and watched the artist continue to paint. He worked most of the day, stopping now and then to talk to other artists and tourists. Before leaving the city, I would buy a painting from him — to remember my time there.

But, as the weeks in Florence passed, to my regret, I found it somewhat difficult to fully squelch the tick-tocking of my brain. I had slowed down; I relished the time lingered over meals; I meandered among the scarves or fruit in the marketplace and didn't fret when I paused. The vendors let me take my time, decide.

When I returned to my apartment, I opened the windows and slept. And later, I awoke — to the hum of a Vespa, the chatter of birds, the vibrant language of the Florentines who passed beneath my window, and it was then that I remembered that I was going home in a few days. When I did, would I be able to continue this subtle, slowed lifestyle? Would I find myself bristling when the food server hovered or brought my check too soon? Would I lose patience with people who wanted things right then, no waiting? Would I find myself taking things for granted, being rushed and hurried along from one event to another, without fully embracing my experiences?

I packed my bag that night, slowly, methodically checking to make sure I had everything I needed for the journey home, and I reminded myself again and again that I would appreciate my life much, much more if I learned to simply embrace what was in front of me.

# 16. Random Crossed Paths

**Karen Lethlean**

*Coromandel, New Zealand*

Over my shoulders were two unconventional long sausage-shaped bags, connected by webbing. After selling an Auckland purchased bike, I'd forced around both islands, to a hostel manager in Christchurch I'd laced my bike panniers together, atop a smaller back-pack giving a turtle like appearance to my baggage construction. When Mike Cogswell, surrealist and miniature ceramic artist, initially gave me a lift into Coromandel Peninsula, he'd certainly remarked my bags were a curio. Stopping in his beat-up little blue car, before infamous precipitous Water Edge Road skirting Firth of Thames, into Coromandel town. Such a nice guy, and so helpful. Right up there with a parade of boy-scout-types dotting my New Zealand solo adventure.

"Where are you going to stay?" He asked

"A friend told me to show up at Barry Brickell's with a bottle of wine."

"Right. Do you know anything about him?"

"No, except my boss spent an artistic internship staying in an old railway carriage while studying art at Uni. Said Barry might accommodate me in those same carriages, if I promise to share traveller's tales and come bearing a gifts, specifically wine."

Wandering back down Barry's driveway, sans wine bottle; unceremoniously rejected, I smiled at Mike's car still parked beyond the gate.

"Did he answer the door?"

"Yes, but basically sent me away." I'd thought being greeted by a sarong-wearing clay-streaked artist would be genesis for a hospitable apprenticeship helping Barry show tourists around his new mini-railway.

Blissfully ignorant of forthcoming artist tantrums while Mike drove around snakes of roads into Coromandel, I contemplated how power poles were constructed in water because road met firth on one side, steep hills on the other. And what about global warming, and impacts from rising sea levels? While my driver, Mike wore his welcoming artist's hat and pointed out Castle Rock, half hidden in mists so synonymous with this — land of the long white cloud.

"When we came here, this was taken as a sign."

Unfamiliar with his symbolism, I asked, "Something set in stone?"

"We'd all walked away from establishment and rejected mainstream. Fresh from Vietnam war protest marches and placard waving, we were enraptured by ambiences of anti-establishment enshrined in this fist-monolith."

Meantime Castle Rock emerged as symbolic to hippies, alternative or artistic types who arrived in Coromandel during the 1960s, building a reputation for a region steeped in creative works, produce and even drug culture communes.

This being my first time in a living, breathing, functioning artist's studio, I likened my experience to visiting a hallowed place. And hovered in doorways, feeling like an intruder. Mike displayed giant surrealist canvases I might get lost in, similar to sinking into a nightmare. These images of throats contrasted with tiny ceramic pots daubed with fish, reminding me of Siamese fighting fish trapped in tiny aquariums. Being surrounded by in-progress art produced a euphoric effect. Even now when I recall wafting aromas of ceramic glazes, oil paints and brushes soaking in linseed oil, stains of the song, A Man of Colours, can drift down. With a whole new meaning because I lived, for a too-short precious time, in this studio.

Those perfect few days spent mostly lazing on Mike's new deck or earning my keep by bottling and cooking warm, sun-dripping nectarines (fresh-picked by my own hands) from Mike's slightly downhill orchard. Scents of jams and pies seeming to compliment various artistic aromas.

"I'm coming out of my cave dweller phase," Mike said. A phase-stift clearly recognizable by partially constructed decks around his tiny A-frame. This coming out also meant my amicable host became impromptu tour leader. Willingly taking his charge to studios, museums and bookshops, I'd never find alone. We explored hidden galleries together.

As Barry didn't feel like opening his Driving Creek railway that week, due to being engrossed with work on giant terracotta figurines I'd been shown as justification for his unwillingness to entertain an un-paying guest. Back then Barry Brickell's 15-inch gauge miniature railway wasn't so well known, therefore he could choose when to welcome tourists, not regulated opening hour's style. You only got to ride if Barry felt like opening his gate! Besides carriages and fittings still functioned as a clay transportation devices, rather than being set up to move tourists about.

Mike even showed me tempestuous east coast surf beaches so contrasting with the low, flat pale greenish-grey waters of Firth of Thames Bay. One cold, windy day, I admired his confidence sprinting out into mountainous waves. Tourism hadn't yet become a big-time Coromandel invader, so it was impossible to secure such insider's perspectives no matter how much I'd been prepared to pay.

All this pleasure resulted from randomly crossed paths.

Chatting in the pub, I became an eager listener to tales of Barry's gossip worthy moments. Every small-town benefits from having such noteworthy individuals. I giggled while hearing of Barry's drunken, naked midnight walk down the town's main street. Much less frightening than my experience in company of another man who disrobed after dark, and strolled nonchalantly along a suburban footpath, "to prove I can." I silently thanked whatever kismet granting Mike, not Barry as my host, and thought someone ought to write a book about Barry Brickell. People openly called him Barry, Mad Potter of 'Mandel.

But now, unfortunately my wistful times were concluded. I was departing Coromandel Peninsula with my thumb pointed toward faster transport.

Dave slowed, to get a closer look. Wasn't until he'd almost overtaken my thumb, that the action registered as a ride request.

"Will we stop, eh?"

The other two grunted affirmations as soon as they saw a female backpacker-hitchhiker.

Their old station wagon pulled over into dusty road edges. At some stage a white car, now mostly grey, pitted by salt spray, daubed by half-finished panel beatings and pink automotive undercoat. Three boys shuffled to make space for a newcomer and bags.

"Where you going?" one asked. Obviously in the same direction, it's really a question about how far.

"Trying to get back into Auckland."

"We're going as far as Hamilton, that's our best offer."

"Great, that's a big help, I can probably pick up a local bus service from there."

Once moving again, I scanned my new situation and took in some details.

Each of these boys were giant Maoris, likely to tip metric scales at 150 kilos, more than 330 pounds. All Blacks front row forward style, wait — man-mountains, a viable description. My driver wore jeans, blue at some stage of their life, now more a shade of greyish-brown. A distinct fishy smell permeated; stains likely to be mud, grease, or fish-gut remnants.

"We've been getting mussels up 'mandel'," one passenger said.

I felt embarrassed, maybe these guys saw my unsubtle response, to their bouquet of marine guts, foreshore, jetty pylons, weed, damp and lingering salt mixed with unwashed body odor. I attempted to blend in with car contents, and establish personal-space boundaries. I noticed arcs of half empty beer bottles up to their lips. All three were taking occasional drafts from brown paper wrapped, long-necked brown beer bottles carefully stashed between their legs.

"Wanna swig?"

"Oh, no thanks."

These three cheerfully talked about their catch, great weather and terrific day. While my glances registered a general flotsam of at least a day's work of a male-bonding. Bare, sandy feet; old weathered shirts, wind ruffled hair; plus rubbish and dirt. This vehicle doubled as a general receptacle. Aside from a lack of neatness and their stink, starting to be less noticeable, nothing was too bothersome. Getting a lift has a way of negating major discomforts.

Then a crunch came with an announcement — "Better get more beer, eh?"

"Yeah, there's a pub here, bro, next right."

I tried to broach drunk-driving dangers, but all that came out is a half-hearted mumble accompanied by a barely noticeable head shake. In my capacity as a freeloading hitchhiker I was not really in a position to make negative comments about social alcohol consumption. I chastised myself for being enough of a snob to think a glass of wine, fireside mixed with talking art, books and local scenery any different from this car cocktail. By now we were in a neat parking area, surrounded by low two plank white fences.

"Wait here." Two of the three occupants left. My company now, big boy, not really sharing as I was squashed into limited back seat fragments. He remained silent, grabbed another couple of mouthfuls and stared straight ahead.

After a few moments he too departed, "wanna take a pit stop…" his last words.

Sitting for moments seemed like ages. I contemplated options. For the first time during this whole five week New Zealand hitching and cycling adventure I felt unsafe. What could go wrong? Rape, car accident, abduction…. just a few possibilities crowded in on a lengthening list. Possibility of a collision, festered as a first option.

How much alcohol had they consumed? How much energy expended dragging up nets of mussels, packing, and toting? Alcohol and fatigue — a toxic mix. I'd seen anti-drunk driving advertisements, I knew about the risks. Even if there wasn't mind-numbing open, straight roads synonymous with road trips back home in Australia.

Yet my driver did seem in control. He might have been used to driving with a booze buzz, even under the influence of a little dope. I heard locals are partial to a smoke of good-stuff, impossible to detect any aromas of evidence, up against strong seafood tangs.

For all my confidence I was still one small, slim, foreign girl compared to these three. Yes, they'd been perfect gentlemen, but I could not guarantee this would continue. Who'd know if I vanished, out here on coastal back roads between Coromandel and Hamilton? I remembered some hitchhiking rules, like never get into a car crowded with drunk men; never hitch late at night; always have an out…. It's now or never.

As I left the car and semi-ran to nearby roadside, I heard a muffled, "…where ya going?" blow back towards me. I looked over my shoulder to see if these boys pursued their catch. Congratulating myself for having averted some dreadful scenarios.

What might be the worst thing? I confused a group of guys watching dust settle around a weird hitchhiker trying to run away, lumbering sausage-shaped bags over her shoulders. They may have expected my flight, or been excited by sights of a panicked departure. All possibilities. Most extreme likelihood, my bloody carcass buried in a shallow roadside grave. Such an outcome just as likely to result from sleeping in Mike's little weatherboard shack high above Coromandel Town. Even now I ponder depths of trust granted my artistic friend simply because we shared something ethereal.

# 17. Half the World

**Frank Light**

*Iran*

It had been a wonderful life, better than I could have imagined — late springs and early summers as a boatman on a whitewater river program for in-trouble youth in Colorado, late summers and early autumns on a helitack unit for the Forest Service in Washington state, and winters in mountain cabins trying to write the great American war novel — for a while. Once a week I'd drive to the local high school and hand over fifty cents for a shower. I'd tramp through the snow to the outhouse. Stints as a substitute meat packer paid the bills between the fire and river seasons but were turning me into a restless vegetarian. The outdoor activities didn't point to much beyond the same simple pleasures going forward, the challenges more immediate than prospective. The novel, in contrast, proved more than I could handle.

To prepare for a next phase, in the late fall of our nation's bicentennial, I responded to a listing in a newsletter for returned Peace Corps volunteers about teaching English as a foreign language. Like the Peace Corps, Forest Service, and river crew, the job paid a pittance plus room and board, but it was in the famously tidy, mannered, and prosperous Land of the Rising Sun. Having never set foot there, I broke out a Coors when my application was accepted. I saw it as a stopgap, and so requested a delay to accommodate a previously scheduled interview for a federal government position that wouldn't become available until a year later, at the earliest. No dice: classes began at a certain date.

Referring again to that newsletter, I pursued another English-teaching job, this one in Tehran. In accordance with the law of supply and demand, it paid ten times as much as the opening in Japan, perhaps because Iran was thought to be hot, polluted, earthquake-prone, hard on women, incommodious, and politically repressed: a Saudi Arabia lite, with Shiites for Sunnis and a Shah instead of sheikhs. Compounding that unfortunate and possibly ill-deserved reputation, the military-industrial employer in this case — a subcontractor for Bell Helicopter in conjunction with the Iranian army — must have turned off more than a few Peace Corps returnees. Two sides to every story, I rationalized. I'd see for myself. Iran could be Afghanistan on fast-forward. At the very least it had trains, helicopters, peacocks, pomegranates, and pistachios.

The subcontractor said I could report after the interview: its employees came and went all the time. If the government turned me down, I intended to stay in Iran long enough to save up for a small piece of the Rockies and explore the American wilderness, maybe even get to that pesky novel when snow or rain argued for indoors by the fire.

First, I had to earn it. Tehran struck this mountain-man wannabe as the Big Apple of middle Asia — brash on the surface, ambitious the next level down. Opportunity knocked most obviously for foreigners, the powerful, and the wealthy, but if you weren't born to it, you could work for it, in some cases scrounge for it, if necessary lie for it. If not for yourself, for your kids.

With new riches came fresh hopes, revived fears, and portents of an order yet to be defined. One Friday, colleagues and I splurged on tickets for an uptown buffet said to offer all the shrimp, sturgeon, caviar, prime rib, and other delicacies a gourmand could eat. The queue inched forward until, finally, it brought us into an aromatic central hallway. By the time we reached the groaning boards, they had been picked clean. Those ahead of us stood gorging themselves on scraps. Everyone ate, from first to last helping, in place.

The following Thursday I was in line for *Star Wars* when a phalanx of police appeared out of nowhere and started thwacking young hipsters in front of and behind me with rubber truncheons. We were blocking the sidewalk, they snarled, a spurious charge. Their blows only seemed random: they spared the foreigner.

Shaken, I skipped the movie and asked for a transfer south to Isfahan. Less city, more soul, a secretary promised. Isfahan had once been the world's largest city, capital of an empire. You could see that in the architecture, things made by man and their relation to those made by God, a delight in opposites, reach against cohesion, the play of space, sky, earth, and water. Nestled against a river crossed by ancient, arched bridges, a vast plaza at its center, Isfahan was beautiful and knew it. Like Paris or, less consciously, Herat, across the steppes in Afghanistan, it basked in past glories. Isfahan is half the world, an old saying went, and everyone knew it.

In an effort to deal with the other half, Bell housed its employees and families in a bedroom community, a Levittown east complete with softball field I'd frequent for slow-pitch games that rewarded men twice my size swatting the ball over the fence with ease. Most employees were Vietnam veterans, with varying levels of adjustment to an alien environment where nobody was out to get them. I never met a one who was into the local culture, though they motored into the city for restaurants, carpets, jewelry, and sightseeing.

Bell had a contract to equip the Iranian army with helicopters and train its soldiers to fly and maintain them. Rather than employ interpreters or train up a few Iranian instructors, Bell gave technical classes in English. That required the students understand English, which is where I and a few dozen other American teachers came in.

The only foreign language our charges knew on arrival was some Arabic picked up at the mosque. Mine were prospective door gunners, crew chiefs, and mechanics, village kids curious about American perspectives, most notably my take on a mad-as-in-angry prophet promoting revolution from exile in Paris of all places.

What? I played dumb to get a rise out of them. Who?

Khomeini, they chirped, almost in unison. The Ayatullah! Repartee delighted them.

Uh-uh, I admonished, wagging my finger, you know we can't go there. Pa Bell's ban on politics was clear. We spoke instead of pitch, attitude, yaw, checklists, and the principles of flight. A highlight was going up for pilot training, the autorotations an airy break from the classroom.

I knew a little Farsi from the Peace Corps in Afghanistan, though Pashtu had been my primary language. That first year I taught English, and the second I worked on emergency drought relief, including in a province on the Iranian border some 600 miles east of Isfahan. I'd look westward and see this same desert, low ridges, haze, and sandstorms.

I could have been there, on the inside looking out, ahead of my time. The Peace Corps offered me Iran or Afghanistan. It was on the phone, late in their season after I had quit my necktie job for a program in Tunisia that was canceled at the last minute, and the busy man on the other end said he needed a decision before we hung up. Nothing else was available. I knew only that on the map and probably in other ways, Iran was between Afghanistan and the West. Afghanistan, I said.

Since I didn't work directly for Bell, I could live in town. After a false start, I settled into an apartment with a cat named Junior and a balcony overlooking a courtyard, the landlord and his family next door. He'd been a civil engineer until felled by a stroke. No longer employable, he found release in crafts, and he gave me an exquisite brass tray he'd engraved with scenes from the city. His wife would bring baklava she baked for special occasions. Their hospitality helped allay the concerns of my parents when they visited. It was their first time overseas.

Most Iranians I met were like my neighbors, warm and welcoming. Not all. When you reached a threshold, say when ten percent of your encounters proved unpleasant, you had to fight a tendency to avoid strangers. Kharajee, a few would mutter as if I didn't know the Farsi for foreigner. Or farangi, meaning Westerner. Kaffir: infidel. They didn't care if I knew they knew. All the better. They found us aloof, or worse — oblivious.

Bicycling to work one morning, I dismounted at the base gate and practiced Farsi greetings with the guard. Bored and stiff in ill-fitting uniforms, his predecessors had appreciated the diversion, pleased to be noticed. This one, a private, responded by saying, "How's it hangin', dude?"

His English was as fluent and colloquial as his opening line. Of Iranian descent, he grew up in southern California and was conscripted while visiting relatives in Tehran. He learned the hard way there was more to the old country than Farsi and family. At first you didn't see it, and then you got used to it.

A follow-up interview for that position with the feds occurred at our embassy in Tehran. Numerous address changes and experiences required a full morning of explanations. The interviewer and I finally got over the hump when we discovered we had each been to Song Be, a bend in the river in Vietnam. Still, decisions were made in Washington. It would be months until I knew anything, he said.

The waiting room for the flight back to Isfahan brought to mind my first time in-country: Tehran, 1970. Our jet-lagged Peace Corps contingent boarded an Iran Air 727 for the final leg to Kabul. Seeing more passengers than seats, cabin crew suggested the overflow stand with hands on seat backs for support, or plop on armrests, or squeeze in next to or on top of already-belted friends. That lasted until the pilot stepped out of the cockpit before takeoff. The extras spent the night in Tehran. The episode showed the awkward fit, marked by trial and error, of technology to tradition, in this case the one for receiving guests.

Another aspect manifested itself on an itinerary that took me to Kerman and Zahedan en route to Karachi. I saved a hundred dollars by going that route and even more by glimpsing enough of those towns to know I'd never return. A traveler needed time — and interaction — to get hooked.

Kerman, I arrived late and left early. The hotel room had been drafty, the walls too thin to muffle the sound of horns, motorbikes, raconteurs, and things (or people) that bumped in the night. Zahedan stood out by comparison, a beneficiary of daylight softened by clouds. As the nearest town to the desolate juncture where Iran, Pakistan, and Afghanistan came together, it might have been remote a decade or so earlier, and it conveyed a potential for refuge if the saplings that lined the avenues were watered and left to grow, but in the winter of '78 it had lost what it used to have and had yet to sense where it was headed. A British couple I met at the airport checked into the government guest house, a bastion of sterility. Although cleanliness off the beaten path was not to be scoffed at, its price — $22 — sent me into town for a better deal.

At a hotel the cabbie recommended, the manager, a type found in Indian comedies — short and round, with a two-saber mustache — showed me a room a Pakistani family had moved out of with such haste they left their sandals behind. I asked why. By way of reply the man directed me to a room he had said wasn't available. Appointed with sink and shower (toilet down the hall), one flickering light, and two beds as concave as cargo slings, it was sandal-free. I surrendered six dollars and my passport.

In need of a dousing, I leaned my head into the shower. The taxi ride had been chilly, the windows unclosable. Daylight rose out of the drain, and I could tell by the jerry-rigged set-up the water would never get hot. The towel I rubbed over my scalp looked to have been washed in a river, dried in a dusty wind. This was a room for someone who would spend his day discovering there was nothing to discover in Zahedan. I could have been wrong, but with the beginnings of a sore throat and another early departure on tap, I wasn't in the mood. I retrieved my passport and six dollars, the manager no longer smiling, hailed the cabbie who brought me — funny, I hadn't asked him to wait — and put up with the receptionist's smirks on my return to the guest house.

I did not travel widely — only Persepolis, Shiraz, and Abadan besides the cities already mentioned — and I didn't mingle as one might expect of a former Peace Corps volunteer. To do that well, your job should require it. Mine didn't. The students lived on base, their barracks off-limits, and townsfolk associated resident foreigners with the military. That didn't stop me from forming opinions, and here's how I saw it: the culture set norms for the upper and lower classes. In the past that's all there was. Then came oil, and the slopes got slippery. Those profiting from it, directly or indirectly, took on the worst aspects of both classes while discarding the best. They paved their gardens to park their cars. Money made them and the things they bought bigger. And louder. It drew those without it to the cities, where anonymity served as a petri dish for change. Influx and disorder, embodied by touts, peddlers, beggars, job seekers, day laborers, country cousins, high-salaried kharajee, and their appurtenances, crowded the man in the street.

Even with the jostling, I couldn't imagine the demonstrations that attracted my students' empathy would lead to the Shah's downfall. The ruins at Persepolis paled next to the lustrous, blue and white remnants of the extravaganza he had hosted to celebrate the 2,500th anniversary of the Iranian monarchy as if his line started then instead of with his father. He had legacy in mind. He wanted to be admired. He was insecure. His health was failing. Whatever. The King of Kings, as he liked to be called, lost his nerve.


For eight months after the follow-up interview I heard nothing. Then a telex arrived giving me two weeks to report, barely time for due notice, let alone a proper reckoning. I sprang for a carpet I had been slow-bargaining for, power-shopped for Persian miniatures, took photos, wished God's blessing on my landlord and students, exchanged addresses with coworkers, and found Junior a new home.

In Washington a "career manager" pushed hard for my acquiescence to a posting in Tehran. Nobody else was interested, and I knew the country. To him, a no-brainer.

To me, a non-starter. My heart and head had moved on.

At least take the Farsi test, he urged.

Trying out my bureaucratic skills, I stalled.

We have to send somebody, he whined.

When asked, I told a fellow recruit Tehran had a lot going for it. Busy, bustling, tolerant, modern yet alive with history. Downtown museums and monuments, nearby skiing, distinctive cuisine, a society in transition if not upheaval, and underneath it all, a vibrant, outgoing citizenry.

In Mexico I learned the Revolutionary Guards had taken him and 51 other Americans hostage, as a new righteousness overturned the old codes. That was November, 1979. In December the Soviets invaded Afghanistan. I saw him only once after that, years later at our embassy in Paris. He didn't have much to say about it, not to me, anyway, giving the impression he too wanted to move on.

I've been back to my first love in the neighborhood but never Iran. I can't say I gave it a fair shot, and now is too late. I can say there's not a place in the world, Kerman and Zahedan aside, I don't miss.

# 18. Mom and the Michoacán Mariposas

**Bridget A. Lyons**

*El Rosario, Mexico*

Dragging my seventy-five-year-old mother to the mountains of Mexico may not have been my brightest idea. This thought metamorphosed into a stomach cramp as we approached the El Rosario entrance to the Reserve. Just because I was obsessed with monarch butterfly migration, didn't mean everyone was.

The ejido's gatekeeper allowed us to proceed to the upper parking lot. "La vieja cojea," our guide had said to him, gesturing to my mother and using the verb that generally describes her condition — dropped foot (which forces her to limp). We were greeted by a mural-smothered concrete arch and a bevy of women hawking butterfly tchotchkes. My mother stumbled out of the back seat. "Whew, I'm having trouble breathing," she said. The parking lot sits at about 9,500 feet. The oyamel trees in which the butterflies congregate sit up above 10,000.

I had wanted to visit Michoacán's Reserva de la Biosfera Mariposa Monarca since I'd moved to Santa Cruz, CA — another spot on the planet blessed with the privilege of hosting overwintering lepidopteral hoards. After living there for a couple of years, I developed a practice I called "butterfly church." This involved arriving at the eucalyptus grove when the insects were just waking up. Every night they come together to form dense clusters, clinging to one another and hanging from tree branches during the cold and wet hours. When the temperature rises to fifty-five degrees, they come alive, one by one leaving their clumps and taking flight. I was captivated by their diurnal cycles, and, in the process of researching their unusual migratory patterns, I learned that the Santa Cruz butterfly scene paled in comparison to the insects' main North American overwintering site — the Michoacán Reserve. I was determined to experience it.

Without giving the conditions much thought, I hastily fired off an email to my mother, saying, "I'm going to see the butterfly reserve in central Mexico. A billion monarchs in one place. Nearby colonial city with lots of famous churches and world-class food. Wanna go?" My mother is, as one of my friends used to say, "game." Over the years, I have taken her to obscure villages in Colombia, remote artisan workshops in the Peruvian highlands, and dusty, overcrowded Guatemalan markets. I knew what her answer would be.

It wasn't until I got to our hotel in Morelia — the large city nearest to the reserve — that I realized the questionable wisdom of my offer. The awkwardly-worded brochure on the dresser reminded me that people who live at sea level struggle with the lack of oxygen in the mountains. It also reminded me that even the most accessible of the reserve's three entrance points requires a three-hour drive from Morelia, followed by a steep and dusty climb into the forest. It could be very hot, very cold, or very rainy, and there was no guarantee that the butterflies will be awake and active on any given day. In its poorly-translated cheeriness, the pamphlet said the trip was "for the adventure-liking traveler in good health." Despite my mother's determined attitude, her condition often impeded her from walking up stairs and ramps at home. I slumped onto the king-sized bed in the room she had paid for and rubbed at the wrinkles burrowing into my forehead. I spent a few hours finding a guide who was willing to work an extra-long day with an uncertain outcome. "I've gotten eighty-year-olds up there," one said. "Ningun problema. We'll just take our time."

During our drive, we passed through acres of dry grasslands, lines of nopal cactus, tidy rows of peach orchards, and small, square fields of blue agave. "Those look like the ones we saw in Oaxaca," my mother said, pursing her lips as she remembered the taste of mezcal. We traversed this agricultural area's main industrial hub, the gritty village of Maravatio — a name that, since it sounded to me like "maravilla" (miracle), I hoped it was a good omen, because after we had driven through that bustling thoroughfare of tire shops, beer drive-thrus, and used clothing stores, we began to climb into the pine forests that characterized the alpine sector of the state of Michoacán. When we stopped for cold drinks and a stretch break, my mother was dragging her leg.

Along the route, there was plenty of buildup to the main event — from monarch murals on school buildings to butterfly icons on road signs. We climbed through the shade to the village of Aporo, with its classic Mexican zócalo, or square central plaza, then further to Ocampo, a town with an inordinate number of topes — speed bumps. "Like we could drive fast if we wanted to?" I said. The curvy, pothole-ridden roads concealed children, dogs, and cattle at every turn. "I'm glad we're not driving ourselves," my mother replied. The same thought had crossed my mind. A handful of switchbacks and a few hundred more feet of elevation later, we arrived at Ejido El Rosario, the part of Ocampo that collectively owns the right to run reserve tours and manages the parking lot we'd found ourselves in.

The Reserve was huge; it covered 140,000 acres in two states. Since up to one billion monarch butterflies overwinter there, they would typically congregate in a few different spots. El Rosario remains the most accessible one, as well as the one with the densest and most reliable concentration of the insects. There are also three other "sanctuaries," as they are called, open to the public between November and March, when the monarchs arrive from all over the North America (except California — those butterflies overwinter on the coast). At the beginning of their migration, they gather in groups of about twenty million to travel through Texas and northern Mexico en masse, covering about fifty miles per day.

Not all monarch butterflies migrate. In fact, only one out of every five generations does so. Most individuals from most generations live for only three or four weeks. They hatch from eggs into caterpillars, metamorphose into butterflies, then lay their own eggs on a milkweed plant and die. All of this transpires in places like North Dakota and New Jersey and Saskatchewan, and this cycle occurs two or three more times before late summer. The insects that are born in August have a completely different life trajectory, however; they're the ones who make the epic southward journey. They live for eight or nine months, alternately flying and resting as they cover thousands of miles to get to their overwintering grounds. There, they spend some time exploring the Mexican pine forest, but more of their days are spent in a metabolic torpor that allows them to be the "Methuselahs" they are often called.

Just beyond the reserve entrance, at the top of a set of stairs, about ten young men and their horses stood, waiting for paying passengers. "We'll be taking these," our guide said to us, before launching into rapid-fire negotiations. A skinny guy with a pencil-thin moustache pointed to my mother and then to the wooden box used to help visitors mount their docile steeds. My mother grabbed my arm. "You're going to have to help me with this. I've never been on a horse before." Right. I should have known that. It took three of us manipulating my mother's leg and rear end to get her up and into the saddle. As the horse started walking, her face went rigid. I'd finally pushed it too far. I took a deep breath and talked about locking the knees, pressing down in the stirrups, and softening the torso.

Once I had a chance to look around, I realized that the narrow-needled pines we'd started among had given way to oyamel — the fir endemic to central Mexico in which the monarchs chose to roost. Beneath the canopy were numerous penstemon-like flowers that bloom in January, serving as reliable sources of nectar for the butterflies. Small springs punctuated the forest, providing both human and non-human residents of Ocampo with year-round water.

After a steep, dusty ascent, we got to a field and dismounted. "Here's where we start walking," the guide said. "Andamos con despacio; no te preocupes," he added, noticing the concern on my face. He reiterated what he'd told me on the phone — that anyone can get there "con paciencia." It was one in the afternoon. There were no butterflies to be seen. My mother looked exhausted.

About fifteen minutes into the walk, I saw a butterfly fluttering over a puddle. As I pulled out my camera, our guide flashed me a scornful expression. My mother looked grateful for the pause, and she bent over to put her hands on her knees and breathe. Group after group of hikers passed us as we plodded up the hill. But, when suddenly we turned a corner and there were about ten butterflies around us — and thirty or forty of them five minutes later — the expression on my mother's face softened, her tightened mouth and set jaw giving way to a smile. I stopped taking pictures when I realized that we were only on the very outskirts of the butterflies' main area, even though I was seeing more insects in one glance than I had ever seen in my life.

Despite the increase in heat, the increase in altitude, and the increase in the frequency of our breaks, the even more rapidly increasing density of dancing, darting monarchs pulled us up the trail. We paused to observe at least a hundred butterflies hovering above a sunny puddle, drinking. "Come on, the main event is up ahead," the guide said.

As we stepped into the "santuario," I was swimming in a sea of butterflies. They were above me, below me, and around me. They dive-bombed left and right, and they so thickly occupied the airspace that I worried my moving hand might hit one. The forest was more orange than green, more butterfly than tree, more frenzy than stillness. I have never felt so surrounded by life.

It was impossible to know where to rest my attention. One moment, I would be looking at a bush on the side of the trail, focusing on three or four fearless individual insects at close range. A moment later, I would look up towards the electric blue sky and see hundreds of silhouettes fluttering frenetically. I looked deeper into the forest, towards the point where they condensed into collective units of thousands — clouds of orange and brown. A closer inspection of those clouds revealed clumps, clusters, capullos (cocoons) — so many that it became impossible to find a branch without one, and so tightly packed together that the sky was obscured. The sound of their flapping wings drowned out conversation and thought.

The only word I can use to describe what I felt in the grove is "awe." Awe of the butterflies' sheer quantity, yes, but also of their grace, their ease of movement, and the simple fact that they were all there in the same place, at once — a dazzling manifestation of biological creativity.

I scanned the group of people silently gathered in the grove until I spotted her. For the first time, I saw my mother as a young girl, experiencing unadulterated wonder. Her head was tilted far back, her mouth agape. Her eyes glittered like the scales of the monarchs' wings in the sun as she shifted her focus from branch to branch and from tree to tree.

"Amazing," she said. "They are amazing."

She walked effortlessly from one end of the grove to another, without once looking at the ground.

# 19. (Motor)Home

**Dheepa R. Maturi**

*Tennessee, USA*

"Ma'am, are you sure you want to take those with you?"

My aunt nodded vigorously, clutching four bath towels in one arm and the leathery Cherokee with the other as she supported her plump form. He watched the remaining ten of us clamber to the water's edge with varying degrees of grace, given that two of our party wore silk sarees, three carried towels, one lugged camera equipment, and yet another held his cigarettes and lighter at the ready. Most of us couldn't swim a lick.

We were going white water rafting.

Three minutes after launch, our towels were sodden and the cameras and cigarettes, jettisoned. My panic-stricken aunt insisted on maneuvering to a narrow side ridge and then scrambled out, whereupon the hapless raft, now freed of substantial weight, shot down the river corridor. Simultaneously, she and her husband stretched their arms out to one another, Bollywood movie style, shrieking each other's names while the flummoxed Cherokee shouted, "Just stay there, Ma'am! Just stay right there!"

Many years I later, I watched *National Lampoon's Vacation*. When they made that movie, they chose the wrong family.

The entire trip was the brainchild of Chandra Uncle, ever the hatcher of bold plans.

Chandra Uncle's family and mine felt a powerful bond from having immigrated contemporaneously, and as distant relatives for whom geographic distance from the motherland had obliterated true familial distance. Of course, it's possible my parents had never considered the relationship distant — after all,

Chandra Uncle's wife was the sister of my father's brother's wife. Without fully comprehending the exact relationship, I'd nevertheless absorbed the fact that we were all close, and his children were my "cousins" as far as I was concerned.

That particular year, our two families were hosting mutual relatives from India — what an opportunity, Chandra Uncle said, for all of us to experience America!

He rented the largest motorhome he could find — I won't say "RV" because it was nothing like the tricked-out luxury behemoths of today — which had a capacity of eight. (There were eleven of us.) We handed our cash to the owner, and, with nary a contract to be signed or a lesson on motorhome mechanics to be imparted, we stepped aboard our vacation-on-wheels, pungent with commingled odors of rug shampoo and stale smoke, ready to hurtle down the highway, separated from the outside world only by four walls of (we were soon to learn) questionable structural integrity.

As unprepared as we were for day-to-day motorhoming, we did have a plan: drive south from Ohio to Tennessee Ruby Falls and the World's Fair; camp, play, and take in various and sundry sights along the way; and then terminate our trip in Gatlinburg before the return journey.

I don't know how the eight adults adapted themselves to the cramped quarters, but we three kids, ages 10-12, discovered and appropriated a small nook with a table, ostensibly to play SlapJack, but instead to lay plans to steal and destroy our uncle's disgusting cigarettes.

Within twenty minutes, before we could administer the torments, eleven heads rose in unison when sounds began to emerge from the engine compartment — bang, bang . . . sputter-bang-bang. That was the first time.

It was not the last time.

Nasty public showers (ten), injuries (four) and vehicle breakdowns (five) aside, this trip was a shining memory of my childhood. Every aspect was an adventure — from sleeping sardine-like in narrow bunks and buying miniscule boxes of detergent to eating breakfast cereal out of paper cups. At the

World's Fair, I proudly ascended the New Technology stage when a boxy robot asked for volunteers, though I think I accidentally broke its skinny metal arm when it asked for a high-five. At one of the fair's country booths, a kimono-clad lady painted my name on a tiny piece of rice, which I promptly lost. I suspected she didn't really know the translation of "Dheepa" into Japanese.

It was an experience of America, an up-close-and-personal foray through a part of this vast and variegated country we had not yet seen. Against a traditional backdrop of mellow Southern accents, Appalachian terrain, and seriously starchy food (we struggled valiantly for vegetarian cuisine and subsisted mostly on variations of potatoes which we sprinkled surreptitiously with chili powder brought from home), we also witnessed America's overlap of cultures — evidenced not only by our own immigrant presence, but also by the tourists at the World's Fair and Ruby Falls and Gatlinburg, all following multilingual tour guides, taking in the sites, and shopping for kitsch.

Looking back, it is also a memory of myself at my most innocent and idealistic. During that motorhome journey, I lived my actual understanding of America: the place to which a person brought her heritage and placed it in the open-armed embrace of an open-minded country, a country that joyously welcomed all. I experienced a natural extension of those beliefs, and I drank in the cedars, poplars, and amber waves of grain, felt welcomed by everyone we encountered, and never once registered a bemused, confused, or hostile glance, though I'm sure we earned more than one.

At that time, even with my brown skin and Indian heritage, I felt 100 percent American. In school, I'd read about and identified with the brave Pilgrims and the courageous Columbus. During the winter concert, I'd proudly belted out cloying verses of nationalistic songs proclaiming that every one of us, regardless of race, religion, or country of origin, belonged in the United States of America.

Admittedly, one incident did mar my otherwise enchanting trip. Chandra Uncle was incapable of passing a sign proclaiming "World's Largest Waterslide" without stopping the motorhome.

The other adults, much wiser after our first water endeavor, firmly passed on the opportunity, but we kids grasped the proffered foam mats and mounted several hundred stairs. What I didn't know was that the World's Largest Waterslide was comprised entirely of concrete, so both of my forearms, reflexively trying to slow my breakneck progress, clamped down and ultimately lost most of their skin. I landed a bloody mess and carried the burns for the rest of the trip, but, more than the pain, I remember my shock — my searing disappointment in what had seemed so welcoming.

During the years following the trip, realities began to counterbalance my understanding in pace with my maturity. Columbus may have been courageous, but I also learned the effects of his behavior and actions on the natives he encountered. I learned that the descendants of English escapees of religious oppression later burned women at the stake, fearful of their communion with the natural world. I slowly grasped the consequences of a country enslaving an entire race, of its extirpating the indigenous peoples.

The same textbooks that fed me this information had a darker side. They referred to my country of origin as ignorant and backward and claimed it would be a miracle if it could ever feed itself. They ignored centuries of colonial rape that had decimated the wealth of one of the richest nations of the ancient world and disregarded its thousands of years of culture, civilization, and philosophy, as well as its colossal contributions to world consciousness by way of yoga and meditation.

My classmates, influenced by equally inaccurate portrayals in the media of the time, asked whether I ate eyeball soup or sacrificed humans or worshipped rats. Some asked me to identify my tribe, though that sort of ignorance hurt less. I'd like to say I quickly and consistently refuted all the erroneous statements and bizarre questions, but eventually, their sheer accumulation made me turn away, shame bubbling. Over time, I became too tired and embarrassed to battle.

It was my most difficult lesson growing up: even if I embraced the people around me as my American brothers and sisters, not all of them would see me in the same light. Rather, they might see only the brown and braided one, whose family members wore dots on their heads, who hailed from a pitiful, primitive place. I began to comprehend racial slurs and to realize they were directed at me. I cringed as kids pretended to pull out the pins of hand grenades, throw them at me, and then shield themselves from the purported explosions. My parents revealed they'd been refused service in restaurants, that they'd received anonymous letters threatening our family and admonishing us to return to wherever the hell we came from.

In college, I studied the instability of recorded history and the ways victors, colonizers, and oppressors harnessed language to tell their stories and characterize their victims. In fact, the precarious connection between history and truth became the subject of my senior thesis, the culmination of the sadness of the ten years following my motorhome journey.

Throughout those years I wondered why many cousins and friends in larger cities, even those just five or six years younger than me, did not seem to face or feel the same torments. Perhaps there were larger numbers of minorities in their towns and schools. Perhaps, within a few short years, popular culture gradually absorbed and displayed sufficient bits of Indian culture to ward off potential assailants — Bollywood dance contests, henna tattoos, brown faces in movies and TV shows, "Jai Ho" piping through shopping center music systems.

I think of my child self, the girl who had the chance to feel and experience her ideals first-hand while roving America in a motorhome. She visits my consciousness from time to time, especially as the country becomes more complicated, its politics more dysfunctional, its race relations simultaneously more nuanced and more incendiary, and as conversations proliferate about who belongs here and who needs to be removed.

She is the one who reminds me of my awe of the social experiment that is "America," an experiment stunning in its scope and its appeal to human nature at its most inclusive and accepting. She recalls my admiration of the forefathers' decision to set standards so altitudinous that achieving them could only be a journey — a Herculean, and perhaps even impossible, one.

And she reminds me of my sheer gratitude for having grown up here, for having received such opportunities and experiences, for having met people so open-hearted, so desirous to learn and understand, and so cognizant of the hybrid vigor and blended beauty of this visionary place. I am thankful, too, for the perspective my life here provides vis-a-vis my own cultural heritage, for the space it grants me to examine and choose the principles and standards that fit my life and my family, and for this fertile, fecund, in-between space I occupy.

My love is no longer innocent, like a child's. Rather, I love this country like a spouse whose failings I must forgive, over and over, whose many kindnesses and virtues I must remember and cherish over our long haul together. And I love it like a parent who honors good intentions and efforts, who believes in potential and promise, and who excuses missteps and disappointments–every time.

# 20. Waiting in the Parking Lot

**Devan McNabb**

*Michigan, USA*

The blue light filter on the phone helps a little, but it's still too bright. An old analog alarm clock slowly tick, tick, ticks, with silent judgement as it winds closer and closer to the time it is set to ring. Just another page, another link, another new idea. My thumb flicks across a screen scrolling through hacks, reviews, and blog posts. It's hard to put the damn contraption down, roll over, and fall into much-needed sleep before another day of work. All these aspirations divide attention in a dozen different directions. The strong Lake Michigan winds hit the blinds making them knock against the window loudly and rhythmically.

Staring up at the ceiling, my mind reels from overwhelming stimulation and it's both the screen itself and its content. The internet is strung up with lively banners proclaiming the sanctity of dream-following and sings out encouraging words — at least in some places. At times, like tonight, it instigates a tightening tension. It's like the alarm clock tick, tick, ticking away towards the eruption of a clamorous, joyful noise. If I sit up in bed I can see my van patiently waiting for me in the parking lot. She's all strung up with thrift store sheet curtains on Cat5 cable. She's outfitted with a plywood bed supported by old school Rubbermaid foot-lockers and never enough gas in the tank. Her tail end is tattooed in a colorful display of some of our adventures: Yosemite, Mammoth Cave, Red River Gorge and places I went without her: Scotland, Spain, Shanghai. Also, a few philosophical mottoes like, "Find what you love, love what you find." The stuck-on emblems are what delineate her from the suburban Honda Odysseys, fetching families to and fro. She's the culmination of late-night internet inspiration and my innovation. The van is out there dutifully waiting through the dark for the leaves to turn a fiery red and orange, for my schedule to change and the opportunity for adventure.

The sun reflects harshly on the metal edge of the window frame, and the alarm clock goes off rocking from side to side in a ruckus. Pulling the blanket up around me to combat the cool morning air, I toss around a vague plan to head out to the DNR land a few miles away on my next free day. Sneaking off into the Midwestern woods recharges social interaction batteries. The short trips solidify the idea that sitting with back hatch open and staring out at the wilderness is a mainstay in my human experience in the story that I'm writing for myself.

# 21. Patagonian Memory

**Kari Nielson**

*The Nef Valley, Chile*

The geometric tract of land where we walked had been plowed clean by a landslide or avalanche. Huemul — a stout Patagonian deer — tracks led us up the hill. In the west, where we came from, the rolling trunk of Glaciar Colonia flowed down a central valley and three of its branches tumbled from surrounding peaks. The origami creases in the surface of the glacier glowed blue, even in the dense morning's gray light. The enigmatic base of Cerro Arenales smudged into the murky sky.

Over the pass from the Northern Patagonian Ice Field, the vegetation thickened. My climbing partner, Joshua, and I made our first right-hand turn in the oval we were to walk around the mountain range, too small and unpopulated to bear a name, though a circumnavigation would take us eight days. We had come to Chile's Aysén region to work on a guide's ranch in a parallel valley. In the previous two days, we had walked north, alongside Glaciar Colonia, to the Nef Valley. We were getting to know the neighborhood.

By midday, we had bushwhacked into old growth forest. Erratic, moss-covered boulders were folded under a twisted canopy. An irrational but tense expectation of encountering other living beings forced me to listen deeply through the silence. Brown songbirds punctured the veil of stillness. They flitted and jumped in pairs. They called out, ordering us to back away from their nests.

We came to an abrupt opening in the trees, which provided a view of the vast valley below where we stood. The hillside abruptly dropped to a wide plain that fed Lago los Ciervos. Joshua swore. No easy route presented itself, and we had to continue straight down the steep mountainside to the flat and treeless valley floor.

I broke through an entangled wall of green and descended into the forest. My perspective alternated from the immediate obstacles of dead trees and holes obscured by stiff ñire branches to calafate spines that dug into my hands. Keeping track of Joshua, a faster hiker, became a separate challenge. I tripped over a fallen tree. I couldn't hear Joshua. I called out and blew into the whistle that affixed to my backpack's chest strap. A tinny voice drifted from far off. Sticks pulled my hair, my pack snagged on ñire. I stopped to listen. We exchanged calls. I crossed back from where I had come, angling toward Joshua's voice. Falling and tripping my way down, we met above a short rock face.

"I think I should go first," I said.

We soon came across a cow skeleton decayed clean down to its white bones.

When I broke into the open plain, it felt like rising through the surface of water. Pulled by the hope of the flat and forested land on the opposite side of what turned out to be an expansive marsh, we picked our way through dead logs, tufts of long green grass, and mossy islets. Dead trees stood like telephone poles. The terrain gradually congealed into moss. Clouds streaked down from the mountains. Joshua had drifted out ahead. He cursed occasionally, and I heard myself doing the same, swinging between exhausted ecstasy and the uncontrollable sense that I was at war with the ground.

A stream with autumn-colored pebbles in its bed marked the end of the marsh. I crossed the stream and crawled under a short arc of branches into another labyrinth of woods. Joshua had disappeared. When I finally broke through the last barrier of vegetation before the lake, Joshua was standing in the rain, watching a pair of brown ducks drifting on the rippling surface. The valley beyond the opposite shore curved left. The horns and needle-point summits of the Ice Field had smoothed over. Snow-covered slopes rolled to the east. The climate became drier as the valley descended.

"We need to stop," I said.

Retreating inland, the forest was surprisingly opened beneath the canopy. As the light faded, we set up camp on the first solid, flat, dry ground since crossing into the Nef Valley. Avoiding the numerous widow-makers dangling overhead, I set up the tent. Joshua toppled dead saplings and started a fire before the rain passed through again. I followed vague cow trails to the stream and filled water. The fire emitted damp smoke. I ate rice and lentils furiously.

That night, I encountered visions of a girl wearing a silky white gown. She stood beneath dripping lichen that draped over gnarled branches. The woods were quiet and nearly lifeless. I listened to the stream that flowed into the lake where we had watched the pair of silent ducks in the rain.

An open space in the dense lenga revealed the first evidence of human life. A collapsed corral lay in the grass, its old gate cast aside. As we stood in the green clearing, it began to rain.

Joshua walked ahead and came upon a trail at the edge of the lake that passed in and out of the water. I was simultaneously relieved and burdened by evidence of humans. I let my boots soak through in the lake.

Just past the eastern shore, we approached a puesto, a ranch camp where gauchos stayed when they seasonally herded cattle and sheep up-valley. A tall pole in the center bore the weight of the sky. Long knotty boards stood upright and wide gaps had formed between them. A fire, likely intended to clear land for grazing, had burned up the hillside, but had left a smattering of gray, charred stumps and standing trunks. Two Crystal beer cans lay crushed, their labels fading, next to a pile of charcoal. A nearby corral remained intact, and a single coigüe tree grew full and broad in its center.

The distinct trail, hammered in from decades of horse travel, unraveled on the hill above the rundown camp. A bluff rolled into a cliff that looked over the milky blue of the Río Nef where it escaped from a narrow slot up valley and released into its wide river plain. Our boots pressed into the yellow muck, leaving streaked prints.

Within several hours, a high vantage revealed a cleared circle of land and an A-frame wood shed lined with fluttering black plastic. A house stood in the center of the grassy property. I noted the rotting shingles and black caves of windows. Water had seeped upward  and left the lowest half-meter of the walls gray. Holes in the walls and ceiling, covered with tattered plastic sheets, left the interior open to wind that shuttled down the valley from the west.

A new brass padlock clasped the door, but loops of wire actually held it shut. Joshua untwisted them before stepping inside. A seam had torn down the roof's ridgeline. The hole let in the rain, so that the particle board paneling of the interior walls bulged in. A half-full burlap sack swayed from the ceiling and freshly cut firewood lay stacked along the wall near the door. A pair of boots with the toes worn through hung framed in the upper right quadrant of the hollow north-facing window. A rusty horseshoe clung to the window's T-shaped center.

Feeling like intruders, we stepped outside. I took care not to step through the porch's rotting floor. The overhang sagged and we had to stoop in order to leave and enter. A child's shoe was wedged between shingles; a faded blue sweater hung from the rafters. From the porch, we could watch light as it shifted in the mountains. Someone had taken such care to split the shakes. A ghostly passion persisted. In the day's wet dreariness, we saw the forces that pushed people out of the valley. Those who went too far, who were too isolated during the storms in the mountains, when the streams were flooded and trails turned to rivers. The intensity of the pioneers' journeys and lives endured in the landscape's memory.

We picked and ate ripening calafate berries next to the open fence. Fragrant mint grew in the thigh-deep marsh that moated off the campo.

Tired after several hours of walking on the trail, we considered camping at a stream that rolled down from the southern mountains, but decided to continue until the next water source. A fence blocked off a small hillside planted with rows of pine. Around the next curve in the mountainside, acres of pine spread beneath the next snow-dusted ridge. The neat rows contrasted with the dense blanket of native Nothofagus forest that remained. The trail followed a clean fence line through the neat geometry of the pines.

The evening sky cleared and we made camp where we could see a cluster of poplars, which signified human habitation. I took comfort in the sound of sheep bleating.

We woke on the high bank and took the morning to dry our clothes in the sun. Sheep trails wound through the choura bushes and occasional pine trees and coalesced at an opening in the fence.

The trail curved down below the high bank where we'd camped and into an open grove of trees. A house, surrounded by poplars, was constructed of a neat conglomerate of shakes and metal roofing. A solar panel faced north. It seemed rude to either knock or to leave without saying hello. I approached the gate in front of the house and called out. "Hola?"

The corner of the curtain swished open, and a face briefly appeared. The door opened, and a woman smiled to show her missing front teeth. Neither of us quite knew what to say. I wanted to talk to her, but hadn't planned on that moment of silence. She seemed kind, and her eyes crinkled when she invited us in. Her name was Elena.

Elena stood in front of the shelves that served as her pantry and next to the wood stove. She monitored the temperature of the water and refilled mate as we passed the gourd around. She wore sweatpants and a t-shirt. Normally wary of tortas, a Patagonian frybread, I happily ate two from the plate that she offered. The fluffy white flour and lard tasted like a doughnut. To express gratitude, I mentioned that Evaristo, our neighbor in Valle Colonia, made tortas that were hard, like rocks. "Es porque el esta solito," she said shortly. It's because he is alone. She meant that he had no wife, and I felt bad for saying anything.

Elena's husband, Don Marco, had ridden to the neighboring valley for a Christmas party. She had opted to stay at home. She normally made the four-hour ride to the Carretera, the highway, once every four months. She strung along two pack horses that carried her home-spun wool and returned loaded with powdered milk, pasta, oats, rice, and mate.

Elena's parents had originally settled in unknown decades before. She was the last of her siblings to live in the campo. Uneducated herself, she had sent her three children to live with their grandparents in Cochrane when they were young. Her cousin owned the pine farm up the valley, an operation subsidized by the government, like many pine farms in southern Chile, in order to combat erosion and provide a fast-growing source of wood for pulp mills. Five years earlier, her cousin had commissioned a team of workers to bring the saplings in on horseback.

A baby goat walked through the open door, its hooves clacking on the cement floor. "Venga, Juanita," Elena cooed, her hand outstretched. Juanita began to nibble at the spinning wheel and wool, and Elena flicked a willow switch that she kept in the corner to shoo her out.

I asked her what she liked about living in the campo. Everything, she said. It's tranquilo and beautiful. We talked about the roads the government was building in the Maitén and Colonia valleys. "Espero que no cambiaré," she said shortly. I hope that things will not change. Her dark eyes glowed, and she no longer smiled.

Elena described her life as "puro caballo," pure horse. She pointed to the tops of the hills that embraced her house. They rolled over into grass-covered plateaus before reaching the snowy alpine. She told us about riding to the tops of those hills when she was a girl. "I have been there," she said.

When we got up to leave after a short hour, Elena asked if we had seen her potato garden on the plateau above the river. Yes, I said, we had. She stood in the doorway and wished us suerte while we loaded our backpacks. I made a comment about how we should have brought a horse.

My feet shifted and dust lifted from the yellow earth. Months, sometimes years, separated the visitors she received in her home. I thanked her again and offered to call her on the HAM radio we had at the ranch. The gate swung open and closed. She waved from her doorstep. When I looked back from the intertwined web of sheep trails that guided us away from the house, she had returned inside and closed the door.

# 22. Prices of Translation

**Paul Perilli**

*Mexico*

¿Voluntad Usted Me Plancha, Por Favor?

There's no surer economic opportunity than a tongue-tied foreigner traveling in your country. Not only was the joke on me, but I'd told it, at a lavadero in San Cristobal de las Casas when I asked the lady at the counter if they ironed? Which would have been silly enough (as I could see, of course they ironed!), but I added to the confusion by phrasing the question as "Will you iron me, please?"

It was a mistake, I knew right away. An international traveler's moment. A moment when I'd lost the ability and confidence to locate the words and conjugations I needed. After I said it, the young woman folding clothes at the big table in back let out a laugh to let me know just how funny I sounded. And a moment later the lady waiting on me quoted a price for my laundry items that, I figured out from the numbers on the board, were somewhat more than I should have had to pay. There was a long pause. The question hung in the air between us. Maybe I wanted to negotiate?

She was right. I didn't. I didn't dare try another sentence.
All that was left for me to do was take the slip she handed to me, say gracias, and get out of there.

## The Two Menu System

My first morning in Palenque I wandered two blocks from my hotel to Restaurant La Canada. Its bamboo covered terrace seemed the perfect spot to eat the breakfast I'd visualized since emerging from a shower. Fresh ensalada di fruta and hot cakes. Coffee too. Several cups, black.

I sat at a small, shady table and ordered off the Spanish language menu. An hour later, I was finished, the plates clean as after a washing, and I made a silent promise to go back the next day.

Nourished, abuzz with caffeine, eager to move on, my waiter, a wide, sturdy man with coal-black hair, set the bill down on the table. Lifting a hip to retrieve the pesos to cover it, a glance at the total made me aware it was more than I was expecting to pay. The amounts for each item were greater than the ones I remembered seeing on the menu I still had a fuzzy view of in my mind. It wasn't the first time that had happened during my weeks in Mexico. But right then I wanted to contest it. This isn't right, it bubbled in me to say. But looking at the waiter, whose eyes seemed focused on a place far away and long ago, the feeling passed.

Forget it, a little voice in my head repeated. And that's what I did, left the amount and a tip without comment and went looking for a collectivo to take me to the temples.

The next morning, Agua Azul in my plans, I sat down to a different menu than the one I'd been handed the day before. This one was printed in English, not Spanish, and had a different set of prices.

So that was it. I had the revelation other Restaurant La Canada customers likely came to before me. They had a Spanish menu for locals with one price list and another for English-speaking tourists with a different one.

The waiter must have seen this flash of interior enlightenment reflect in my eyes, and the change in mood that came over me. He took half a step back as if to give me room to think about what to do next. Ask for the Spanish menu? I could do that. But what if he shook his head no? What would I do then?

My Spanish wasn't good enough to discuss the matter with the thoroughness and diplomacy it would require. I was reluctant to contest it, and I didn't. Instead, I ordered ensalada di fruta and huevos a la Mexicano. After eating I left the amount and a tip and went on my way.

Back at my hotel later that evening I justified my inaction and the two-menu system as the price of translation and left it at that.

The next day I went back to Restaurant La Canada. Paid the English language prices too. Left a generous tip. And that pleased my waiter very much.

## The Shoeshine Kid

In Oaxaca, I was eating at an outdoor table on the zocalo when the kid approached me and stopped, his words bursting forth in very good English.

"Mister, you want your shoes shined. Five pesos, mister, I shine your shoes. Okay?"

It didn't matter I didn't answer him right away. The kid with the San Francisco Giants cap, too big on his head, squatted and set up his kit. A rag draped over two fingers was ready to dip into the tin of tan polish.

"Sure thing. I'll give you ten pesos, but only if you do a good job."

"Okay mister, that's what you get, a good job." The kid looked up and smiled. "A good job for ten pesos. No for fifteen. Sorry mister, I make a mistake in my prices."

After traveling a week in Mexico I'd seen an entire army of boys with their shoeshine kits set up on the streets offering their services, and I'd hoped it was an occupation that supported all of them. This one finally broke me down, and maybe he saw in my eyes I was ready to give in? He rubbed and buffed my leather hiking shoes with zeal. He was used to hard work, I saw. Maybe eleven or twelve years old, I was sure he was in training for a lifetime of it.

When the kid was done I counted out the fifteen pesos he wanted, not only for the good job he did but for his impressive business skills as well. In fact, I thought it possible he knew more languages than English and Spanish. His clientele was an international one, after all. He made money by making personal connections with them.

When I handed him the coins I was pleased to see the look of surprise on his face. Without another word he went off looking for his next customer.

# 23. Monsoon in Kolkata

**Anitha Devi Pillai**

It was during a monsoon rain
that I had first met her —
the Indian Queen of a colonial past.

She lay bare, soaked.
Holding my image of her
in her four arms.

In one arm she cradled
poets and writers who
lay at her feet at College Street,
basking in her warmth, as
she did in theirs.

She cloistered her colonial past
in buildings and trams,
railways and colleges
and held them loosely
in her second arm.

The third was full of vigor.
Flowing Ganges and Kalighat
who were filled to the brim and spilling over
with a million scents for the nose.
But they always made her smile.

Her fourth was her favorite.
Her pride and joy
her children of science and arts
whose fame was scattered across the oceans.
She held them close to her Bengali heart.

Time had stood still for her
as she washed away
the daily grind of the busy city
from her glistening midnight skin.

# 24. The Gravity of Free Fall

**Anna Reid**

*New Zealand*

Our legs dangled over the side of the airplane. Fifteen thousand feet below, the rugged mountains of New Zealand waited to swallow us whole.

Alan tilted my chin toward the exit camera, pressed his chapped lips against my cheek and snapped a photo. Our bodies were strapped together tightly, his familiar heart beating calmly as mine pounded. He leaned forward and we were sucked violently into the atmosphere. I should have been terrified, but the only thing I could comprehend was that Alan had turned my head toward the sun and was kissing me again.

We fell, somewhere around 120 miles per hour. Air filled my lungs. As we raced through the atmosphere, I became acutely aware that being fully alive meant an imminent collision with death. Alan deployed the parachute and steered us to the landing spot. I adjusted my googles then clung to his leg, the only thing within my reach. A primal scream escaped from deep within me. As the ground grew closer, it became clear the rush would end. The finality seeped into my soul like a poison.

I'd never been more certain our intimacy would not last.

ii

Our ancestors used celestial bodies to measure the passage of time. The daytime hours were counted by the shadows cast by the sun, the nights tracked by the Big Dipper and North Star.

I have stood in the Irish countryside as the sun warmed the stones of Newgrange. I have sailed on a yacht under the bright glow of the Southern Cross. I have watched the sunset over Ayres Rock in the Australian Outback. Still, most of my life, I have measured the minutes by the hands of a clock; days by turning the pages of a calendar. It wasn't until this freefall that I began to understand time is measured in two ways: Before Alan and After Alan.

iii

When we first met, I thought Alan was strange. A few chance encounters grew to a few organized ones and I discovered that he wasn't strange at all, just a complex coil of rope that needed to be carefully unraveled. Like a postman delivering the mail, Alan earned his paycheck as a skydiving tandem master, strapping himself to countless people as they checked off their bucket list. It was monotonous work. Apply sunscreen. Grab a rig. Shake hands with the tandem. Fly. Jump. Land. Repeat. On clear days, there were over a dozen jumps by sunset.

On our first official date, Alan took me to a small gallery on the edge of Taupo, a tiny New Zealand town I intended to pass through quickly. Brightly colored mosaic tiles and quirky art were displayed on the walls of the adjacent café. We ordered flat whites and eggs on toast. He walked with his hands in his pockets. His eyes were mysterious, melting into a color somewhere between black and gray. His cheeks turned rosy when he laughed.

Before my last sip of coffee, he had grown on me.

When he drove me home, he slid a UB40 disc into the CD player, skipping to song number five. Higher Ground. This is the song they will play at my funeral, he said casually.

Alan lived in a house nicknamed the Wolf Den with a roommate, Frosty, an IT consultant by day, a co-conspirator of expeditions by night. On the previous census, they had both listed their religion as Jedi and Jehovah's Witness visited frequently in feeble attempts to convert them. They ate fresh venison and blue cheese for dinner, paired with a red wine if there was a sale at Countdown market. Alan would walk barefoot into the supermarket to buy a case, half merlot and half cabernet.

They practiced sheep whistling while a video projector beamed a dancing Michael Jackson on the living room wall.

Sometimes Alan and Frosty would adventure into the early hours of the morning, headlamps illuminating their paths. Sometimes, they would turn in, sober and early, only to dream of the sky. Got to make a living tomorrow, he would text. It's going to be an early night.

Quickly, I learned that it was the extreme of the extreme where Alan found complete freedom. On a small, spiral bound notebook tucked away on a sloping bookshelf, he recorded the details of what made him truly come alive.

A number corresponded with each encounter with mortality.

When I met Alan, that number held at 740 BASE jumps.

Building.

Antenna.

Span.

Earth.

I didn't even know was BASE jumping was when I met Alan. Now I know it only as an acronym for death.

I once asked Alan if he was scared, even after so many jumps. Fuck yeah, Anna, I'm terrified, he said. But I do it anyway.

iv

It was never a secret that BASE jumping was Alan's first love. I was only his mistress. My feelings for him were like carrying an umbrella – mostly inconvenient, completely unreliable, a burden at times; but a shelter I could never resist when the rain came.

Once, I woke up well after midnight to a text. I rolled out of my bed and into a cab he had dispatched. Despite the late hour, music blared from inside the Wolf Den and the front door was uncharacteristically locked. I shivered as I shielded a reusable grocery bag packed with a spare T-shirt and toothbrush. I knew the extra key was hidden somewhere underneath the grill, but instead of searching for it, I trudged around to the back of the house, banging on the windows. I rounded the corner and there he was, completely nude, with nothing on but a headlamp. The dull glow revealed an ax that dangled above his head and he grunted heavily, splitting the damp firewood that would keep us warm through the early hours of the morning.

We pulled his mattress in front of the fire and he'd held me under the plaid comforter. Alan whispered fantasies into my ear, proving there was indeed a beckoning world outside of his death. He would marry me. We would leave the Wolf Den and stay in a real house. We would have a daughter named Keyvie and we would teach her Southern slang. He'd be a pilot so he could still fly from the safety of a cockpit instead of the uncertainty of a wingsuit.

When he would disappear for days, sometimes weeks at a time, I was alone, left to wonder if I had dreamed these confessions. Alan was a man who accepted he would die before he grew up, giving little consideration that a future existed in the air surrounding him.

v

This was the air I gasped as I tried to live life around him.

This air was where I waited for my turn for his affection.

This air was my purgatory.

This air that would eventually kill him.

It was immigration that sealed our fate. Six months after I naively sipped coffee at the art gallery, my New Zealand visa was set to expire.

I wanted more, more of everything, but Alan only had room for one lover.

On our last night together I was painfully aware this was goodbye. I tried to secure the fragile validations of his feelings for me.

I love you, he'd said, as we stood in the Wolf Den's pantry searching for more wine. He gathered my curls at the base of my neck. I remember the first time I saw you. I asked you if you played the Tennessee Flat Top box. Your hair was like this. He looked away, but pulled me closer. I've loved you since then. Since that very moment, Miss Tennessee.

~~But I am going to die. You should know this.~~
(These were the words I could not erase.)

His confessions were glass that would crack before dawn. Within a few days, I'd fly back to America and Alan would carry an urn from his dusty hutch to the South Island and BASE jump his friend's ashes off a cliff.

We loosely planned to meet again stateside. His summer would be spent trying to stay one step ahead of the police as he jumped his way through America's national parks. I would be on an adventure of my own, traveling across the country with a tent, hiking shoes and a plastic cooler crammed in the back of my CRV.

Our paths would cross somewhere, assuming fate allowed. But once again, immigration intervened. Alan would be going to Switzerland, his traveling companion unable to secure a United States visa for entry. Next summer I am coming to America, he wrote in an email. No matter what.

Secretly, I wondered how could I spread my wings when the air around me was purgatory?

I didn't ask. I just waited.

vi

I spent five weeks traversing the States and eventually emerged from a short stay in Yosemite Valley. For the first time in days, a spotty cellular connection allowed a flurry of emails to flood my phone.

Suddenly, I am back on that airplane, hovering somewhere in the stillness of time. My legs are dangling over the side, my knuckles are white and my is heart racing. This time there is no smile, no kiss, and no heart beating behind me. I am plummeting again, alone with no parachute. I hear myself scream which is impossible because the air tastes like poison and it chokes me as I fall, the entire earth waiting to swallow me whole.

Alan is dead.

I do not ask questions.

I do not want to know that his wingsuit has collided with a cliff in Switzerland.

While his family makes arrangements for his body to be brought home from Europe, I board a flight from Los Angeles to Auckland. I rent a canary yellow car and go to his hometown, where I attend his funeral.

After it's over, I drive to the Wolf Den where I am alone. Frosty assures me the key is still under the grill. I use it to open the creaky front door. It is quiet, cold. I don't see the spiral notebook that records his jumps on the sloping bookshelf, leaving me to wonder what number killed him.

I try not to touch anything in his bedroom except his jumpsuit, sparsely hanging in his small closet. I can't help myself as I take the cuff into the palm of my hand and beg for Alan to come back. When he doesn't, I beg for him to take me away. Neither of these things happen.

A week later, I fly back to California, climb into my CRV and leave Los Angeles just after dawn.

The clock and the calendar both read After Alan, and I will eventually remember how to recklessly love again. But, for now, I don't know what to do, so I roll down the windows and slide UB40 into the CD player programming number five to play on repeat. Recklessly I drive toward the Grand Canyon. I think he would have liked it there.

# 25. Swimming in Salt

**Harriet Riley**

*Sydney, Australia*

It's 6 a.m. on a beach north of Sydney, Australia. The sun inches over the horizon, shooting sparks of orange and yellow into the new day. My husband and his two sons stand in silhouette with the rising sun around their bare backs. Boom! A giant column of water hits their bodies. The three determined males dig their feet into the slim wall between the ocean and the pool. The air is filled with the smell of fish and salt and seaweed. The only sound is the crash of the waves pounding the wall and splashing around them into the rock pool.

The three stand, facing the Pacific Ocean on a narrow concrete wall clinging to the heavy iron chains separating them from the huge advancing waves. The rusty thick loops are strung between waist high steel pillars lined along the wall. Behind them sits the man-made rock pool carved into the ancient stone cliffs. In front is the endless ocean at dawn.

This tradition of going to the rock pool at high tide is passed from father to son to son. They wake up before sunrise on a summer's day in January for the drive to Newport Beach to hold onto the chains and let the surf pound their bodies. My husband, with no care for the danger, did this when he was seven. He took his older son when he was young. Now he and his 30-year-old son are bringing the much younger one at age 12 as a rite of passage. The conditions have to be perfect — high tide for maximum wave height and the rock pool in Newport — for this specific position directly facing the Pacific.

These men in my life practice this uniquely Australian ritual. The tide, or rock pools are a special feature in this part of the world. The Sydney area beaches have at least 30 of them, also called ocean pools or sea baths, carved in the rock along the ocean. These pools — ranging in size from small to Olympic length — were constructed beginning in the late 1800s to protect swimmers from shark attacks and riptides. These small bodies of water are tucked away at the either end of most of the beaches. Constructed out of the rock usually with cement, the pools provide smoother water to swim in, flushed full at high tide. Each pool is unique. Most are free for the public, though a few charge a small fee. Visitors include Olympic swimmers in training to small children navigating the water for the first time.

My husband, a native of Sydney, described this beach culture to me, a native Mississippian, before I visited Australia for the first time. He told me stories of the tide pools. They were as big a part of growing up to him as the kudzu, which grew along the highways of my Mississippi childhood, was to me. His grandfather promised each child a new wristwatch for swimming the length of the tide pool at Palm Beach, where the family had a beach house. As the oldest grandchild, he was the first to transverse the pool and win the coveted watch and the pride that came along with it.

His older son — born in London, raised in America, currently living in Sydney — now has the grandfather's wristwatch and the distinction of being the oldest grandchild in this generation. The younger son is American born and bred, but can stomach the disgusting Vegemite as only a real Australian can. Now he is trying to really prove his heritage by passing the test of letting the surf pound his young body at sunrise. He was born for this Australian ritual.

Among the Northern beaches, rock pools to visit include Newport, of course, but also Palm Beach, Avalon Beach, Whale Beach, Mona Vale. Then in Sydney, local favorites are Bondi, Bronte, Coogee, Clovelly, among others. Each pool has its own distinct personality and you have to find your favorite. At all these pools, you'll see the dedicated daily lap swimmers in the water at sunrise all year and the splashing families in the afternoons in the summer.

Some of the first rock pools built in Sydney in the late nineteenth century were in Coogee, Bronte, and Bondi municipal beaches. Newcastle and Wollongong pools were older by several decades, but these city ocean pools had an early influence on Australia's beach and swimming culture, as well as the surf lifesaving movement, according to my research. These early rock pools had restrictions on mixed gender swimming. Coogee Bay even had a women's pool on one side and a men's on the other. Waverly set different hours for men and women. Swimming clubs were formed in the early pools along with competitions and carnivals started which still continue to this day.

Surf lifesavers clubs, another unique Australian tradition, were formed officially in 1907 and helped to develop pools at many beaches that didn't already have one. The pools became training facilities for the surf lifesavers and provided more access to safe swimming when these volunteer lifeguards were not on duty. A wave of new pools were built at Sydney beaches between the world wars and gender-segregated swimming ceased at all locations, enabling women to train for swimming competition along with the men. Lights were also added at several pools for nighttime swimming. In the postwar years, many larger, public in-ground pools were built for year round swimming but the ocean pools remained recreational swimming playgrounds for all ages. To this day, families and swimmers alike enjoy these unique pools along the Sydney beaches.

The chill of the water braces my husband and his sons as their bodies become warmer with the rising sun at the edge of the rock pool. Pleased with their adventure and invigorated for another summer day, they strut back along the pool wall raising their arms in a collective fist pump. The tradition has been completed. They feel strong and invincible.

# 26. The Sidekick

**Shelli Rottschafer**

*Valdez, New Mexico*

I pull out of my driveway. The cooler rests in the well of the passenger side. My hiking boots stand at attention behind my seat waiting to be strapped on my feet. And Makeda, my canine child, is loaded in the back.

Together we are on a road trip; the journey to find calm. Makeda is there because she is my companion. Her unconditional love bounds toward me when she looks over her shoulder to make sure I am behind her.

On one of our first stops, I pull into a scenic picnic area at a reservoir. We have crossed over the Colorado state line into Váldez, New Mexico to take a break from the hum of the rubber wheels on asphalt. The afternoon breezes in the monsoons which just finished pouring.

Once I open the hatchback of my white Subaru Outback, Makeda leaps out and, eyeing the water, she wades in knee deep. The reservoir reflects the periwinkle sky and the Caldera Mountain range surrounding the pond. Its mirror is broken with the ringed wavelets of her footsteps. She laps the water. Her long pink tongue scoops the liquid. Her ribs sigh in pants after her sequester in the car. Back on the shore, she shakes, her black water-soaked skirt shrivels to expose twig-like legs.

I continue beyond the pond, walking toward a mowed meadow. Cattails and water reeds line the shallows beside me. Ranchers have brought their cows here to pasture. Just as I realize the cattle must have been herded down to be watered, a waft of something ripening in the sun reaches my nostrils. I turn to put Makeda on her leash. It is too late.

She writhes on the ground, smiling in ecstasy. I yell a slow motion, "Noooo!!!" and grab her by the collar. "Dammit, Keda!"

I drag her to the shallows and wash off what I can. Like many female dogs, she basks in the rank. Back in the car, her funk fills the cavity of the vehicle. At this moment, I remind myself, "I love her. No matter what."

I am in mourning. Mourning the loss of a relationship is like mourning a death. Tears spring at unlikely moments. I realize I am going through the different stages of grief. I am long past denial. I have let go of the anger. I no longer want to bargain. The depression is moving toward acceptance. My hope is that I will encounter my old self, my true self, on the road like an old acquaintance that I have left behind.

I reach Taos later that day, before the five o'clock cocktail hour rings. Laury waits for me. It has been over a year since I have seen her. Before we allow Makeda indoors, I douse her with doggie shampoo. She wriggles to avoid the chilly hose water that parts her hair, exposing white skin. I scratch in the lavender-smelling goo. She is none too happy, and inches away the cleanse. As I bathe her, I wonder if this road trip will wash away my pain. Will the miles and reconnections be a cathartic respiration allowing me to let go?

That afternoon, Laury and I catch up. I happily climb in her wagon as we tour about town running errands. We stop at a friend's Airbnb. We indulge in fresh squeezed lime margaritas. It is dark by the time we return home. Makeda hovers at the front door, ready to be let out to do her business. I put her flashing red light clip to her collar and she launches into the darkness. Because she is black she blends in; only her arching flashes confess her location in the yard.

Our evening is not quite done. Laury needs to go to the acequia madre. The mayordomo of the irrigation ditch has released the key from upstream. It is Laury's turn to open the gate, flood her back field so that the grass will turn green, the peach tree blossoms will spring, and the parched ground will have her fill. To disperse the water, Laury, and her mother, Mary, tunneled lines throughout the backyard trickling from the orchard patch to an outcropping of flowers and beyond to the grassy knoll.

Since it is the first time this month that anyone has been up to the house, the tunnels lay blocked with pine needles, grass clippings, and other debris. Laury grabs a shovel, and I a hoe. We rake the water through, pushing it along its path to inundate the brittle green. Makeda looks on as she watches her two humans playing in the wet. She sits observing our labor, the red light reflecting in the pool of water. She stands to attention when I leap across the ditch to work the other side of the trough. The toes of my hiking boots glisten in the moonlight from my vigorous scrapping. Laury tries to navigate the jump as well but her legs are not quite as long, and our margaritas leave us less than sure footed. She falls face forward, chest deep into the mucky arroyo. I cackle at her misstep.

"Oh my god Laury, I think I just peed." We laugh hysterically, ending the evening giggling off to our beds.

To be honest, this road trip is something altogether different. In actuality, I am mourning something else that I have not verbalized to anyone. Before I left on the trip, my doctors diagnosed me with an abnormality in my breast. They gave me the permission to go on this trip, one last hurrah, before I go in for my biopsy. I anticipate the verdict with dread. The unknown puts into question my mortality. The doctor's suspicions preemptively give me the permission to say, "The hell with it. I am going to do what I want."

And what I want right now is to satiate my craving, that wanderlust that has long been neglected. The Four Corners is one of my special places. It is the place I feel grounded. I discovered it so long ago while working at a camp outside of Creed. Durango is home to Fort Lewis College, the Durango - Silverton Narrow Gauge Railroad, and Steamworks Brewing Company. Here, my friend Faith has a condo within a stepping stone of Purgatory, a ski area in the San Juan Mountains.

Faith and her girls welcome Makeda and me as we pull into the wildflower-lined driveway. I always enjoy time spent with Faith, Marin, and Dylan. Faith inspires her namesake in others. Her girls provide me with the proud moniker, Tía Shelli. They are two of the precious ones in my life who give me the chance to love maternally. Something that time, age, personal decisions, and health have made not possible.

Faith inquires, "How is everything going?"

I have confessed my upcoming biopsy. It seems safer to tell my kindred spirits who live afar rather than those who are close to home. She notices my worry. Her mom passed due to cancer. She understands the dreaded C.

The following day, our group of five heads to Purgatory Bluff. We pile into the Subaru, Faith and me in the front. Dylan and Marin midway and Makeda enters through the hatchback.

Our hour climb leads us up to a precipice, which overlooks Lake Durango, Electra Lake Reservoir, and Lizard Head Peak toward Telluride. When we reach the top, we all look out. Woman, child, canine. We sit on a log overlooking the view. Makeda nears, she sniffs the peanut butter Power Bar that I extract from my CamelBak. She sits dutifully, anticipating a morsel. I split the bar into pieces, offering it like a communion wafer to toast our success.

We ladies look on in silence, each lost in our own thoughts. Mine travel to the upcoming biopsy and the scars that would put my femininity into question. The future diagnosis would test my understanding of identity. But before that could arise, I turn from my fears to notice my sidekick licking my shin, tonguing up the saltiness. And Faith announces to the girls, "It is time to travel back down to the car."

# 27. Esperanza

**Jonathan Sapers**

*Rincon, Puerto Rico*

On the beach in front of my mother-in-law's house in Rincón, Puerto Rico, are three almond trees. When we arrived to visit in February, months after Hurricane Maria had devastated the island, the trees, which were badly hit during the storm, seemed to still be in a defensive crouch. Their limbs looked contorted, but everywhere, seemingly on every branch, were leaves.

Looking at the trees one had the distinct impression one was looking at what the world will be like in warmer places if we continue to fail to address global warming. The trees will morph into dragons.

The island's beaches are as beautiful as ever. But they appear to have been rearranged. Huge felled trees had been tossed like sticks and buried in sand; other trees had had their tops ripped off. The currents had moved the sand so that it was still smooth and beautiful, but eerily unfamiliar: higher in some places and lower in others, like a captured wave.

My mother-in-law's best friend jokes that as she watched the storm hit, through a side window on the second floor of her cement house, she hoped that she would lose her mango trees, because she had too many and her yard is routinely filled with hundreds of mangoes no one wants. The hurricane took her other trees instead. Leticia, who is in her eighties, rode out the storm alone, with only the radio for company, listening to mayors in neighboring towns being interviewed. "It's bad," she remembers one saying. "Very bad."

There was similar resilience in the voices of many people we talked to, but as in Leticia's case, there was also palpable PTSD. A surfing teacher, Issa, seemed still exhausted by life in the storm's immediate aftermath. He and his wife had gotten up at 5 or 6 each day in order to wait in line to get gas, do what they had to do during the day and return in time to visit his parents and make sure they were safe, before getting home by curfew. Another surfing teacher, Justin, described in detail what it was like to cook lizard. He and his family had lived on canned food and made phone calls using a repurposed car battery.

There was a feeling of nostalgia for the sense of community following the storm, familiar to New Yorkers who were in the city after 9/11; but there was none of the accompanying sense that anything significant was being done about the disaster. Or that there was any reason to believe the island would be any better prepared if it happened again.

After the storm, Leticia had a solar panel put on her roof which she says takes care of some of her electrical needs. She showed us the nest of knobs and dials newly established in her downstairs apartment. She told us that after the storm, many people were unable to use their solar panels because they had blown off and there was no one available with the expertise to put them back on.

During our visit, her friend Nestor, a professor who promotes Puerto Rican artists, came by. He plans to create a poster with a grasshopper on it — esperanza, the Spanish word for hope, is also the Puerto Rican word for grasshopper. But neither he nor Leticia were sure there was much cause for hope given the lack of support from the federal government.

My wife's cousin, Yamil, a doctor, and his wife, Maria, a school librarian, have chosen to remain on the island with their two children. His mother and father and sister left a few years ago, like many people from the island, for Orlando, Florida. His brother is an anesthesiologist and lives with his wife in Arizona. Besides being a doctor, Yamil has become something of an amateur weatherman.

In the aftermath of the storm, Yamil has also been helping with the recovery, working with the Mayor in his hometown of Guayanilla, distributing water and food. The town has a river that is famous for flooding. In the wake of the hurricane, he says he met with a delegation from the U.S. Army Corps of Engineers to talk about the need for a wall around the river to protect local residents from the floodwaters. But according to Yamil, the corps representative was concerned about the environmental impact — in particular on a certain native frog that lives in the river. Yamil was incredulous. "The frogs can swim," he remembers saying. "The old people living around the river can't."

During two trips to Rincón, the first in February, the second in March, our experience of the island's recovery was definitely mixed. On the drive into Rincón from the airport in Aguadilla, power lines along the highway appeared to have been jerry-rigged, doubled up in some places, as if someone had patched together a solution and gone home. On the side of the road from town to our house, what looked like a transformer appeared to have fallen to the ground and been left there wrapped in a snarl of wire. Further along wires hung down by the side of the road, as if they'd been cut.

We experienced our first of three blackouts during a visit to a wonderful new restaurant called Mangia Mi, just off the main square of Rincón. Mangia Mi was started by a couple from the mainland who told us they made it a priority to employ local people who they then train. They say all of the local young people currently working in the kitchen were hired as high school seniors, and have worked their way up from dishwashers to being able to run the kitchen when the chef is away.

Both owners were on hand. One was the chef while the other handled host duties. One of the owner's mothers was visiting and had taken on the role of pastry chef. She had just begun whipping up the frosting for what would turn out to be an incredibly delicious cake when the power went out.

Emergency lights came on and the staff calmly began explaining that they wouldn't be able to take credit cards. Five minutes or so later the power came on again and the mixer went back on too covering the Mom's apron in frosting.

On our second visit we experienced a blackout that lasted an entire afternoon. After an hour or so, I went out to find out what was happening. At the liquor store, the proprietor was resigned. "They don't say — they cut it and then…."

A man buying a case of wine told me I shouldn't worry. "It will probably be over in a few hours."

At Edward's supermarket, the prevailing theory was that there was something wrong at the power plant. "Happens when there are a lot of people here," a man explained. (Visitors had already begun gathering for a surfing competition planned for that weekend.)

Outside Shipwreck, another local restaurant, a man stood chatting with a couple in a pickup truck. Their theory was that there had been a fire in a substation.

"They'll fix it pretty quick," one of the men said.

I went home reassured and the power came back on not long after I got there. The third blackout was happily only a few minutes long. In such a beautiful place, and with people who seem so reassuring, it is easy to see this as recovery. But it's not. People are learning to live with a situation that is unacceptable and untenable. And beneath the resiliency is a sense that there is nothing anyone can do.

Under a more enlightened federal administration, Puerto Rico would seem to be the perfect test case for how to respond to global warming. The government could create an electrical Marshall Plan, modernizing the grid instead of just rebuilding it and providing solar panels. It could help with reforestation — reportedly one of the best ways to protect an area during a hurricane.

Instead, the newly appointed education secretary, mimicking her federal counterpart, is pushing charter schools. Here is a place with a wealth of teachers leaving for the mainland along with so many other Puerto Ricans. Attempting to dismantle the system does not seem to be the answer.

There is hope here, and resilience, but there is also fear. Hurricane season comes in August.

"If another one comes, I don't know what I'll do," said Yamil, possibly at the limit of his patience. And that is reason to worry.

# 28. A Basket Case

## Jonathon Smulian

*Caracas, Venezuela*

In the late 1960s the city of Caracas resonated by day and by night with the sound of heavy freeway traffic, blaring commercial loudspeakers and a cacophony of sirens and car horns. The city's location in a narrow Andean valley seemed to retain and even accentuate every sound. This booming oil financed capital was one of the noisiest cities in South America.

It was a long weekend and a welcome opportunity to escape to the peace and quiet of the almost uninhabited interior of the country.

With two Venezuelan colleagues I left the city in the early morning and drove the Volkswagen station wagon south east towards the *Amazonas*. After crossing the mountain range that surrounded the city we drove for hours over the *Llanos*, the vast tropical grassland plain. Few vehicles passed us in either direction and apart from large herds of cattle, cowboys on horseback and a few lone *haciendas* in the distance we saw few signs of any permanent settlement.

Then in the distance, crossing the flatlands, we saw the Orinoco River in full spate, some two miles wide, glinting in the strong sunlight. Our road terminated at the ferry landing which was in a small village of painted wooden buildings with rusty corrugated iron roofs and rickety front porches. *Cantinas* blared out loud *cumbias and* poorly stocked shops were plastered with peeling advertisements. At the ferry, waiting down river transportation, a huge mound of sacks was stacked on the jetty leaving little space for any vehicle to pass.

The ferry, a battered wooden platform, was only large enough for one vehicle. It was powered by an outboard motor and manned by a crew of two. It had just docked. With the speed of the flow and the logs and debris floating downstream we wondered if that motor was powerful enough to make the crossing. Overturning or sinking was not an attractive idea as the river was the home of shoals of piranhas. With great trepidation I drove onto the ferry platform. The "captain," a wizened barefooted man with a torn shirt and vaguely nautical cap seemed perfectly confidant that he could make the crossing.

After the ferry had been driven sideways a number of times by the force of the flow, and the "captain" had countered by revving up the motor to correct the drift, we eventually reached the opposite bank. Thankfully we landed and drove onto to a poorly defined narrow corrugated gravel road. Towards evening, after an hour of slow driving avoiding the potholes, we reached our destination.

The pueblito of the indigenos consisted of a long hut surrounded by five or six smaller structures. All had roofs of dried reeds and were open on all sides. A row of wooden poles supported the roof of the main structure. A gap in the middle of the structure funneled the smoke from a cooking fire. Some parts of unidentifiable animals hung drying out on a crude wire frame. About twenty people, men, women, and children seemed to live there. Some men, the few that spoke broken Spanish, wore brightly colored shirts, shorts, and baseball caps. The rest wore loincloths and beaded ornaments. A few goats, scrawny dogs, and small children wandered freely about.

From the poles that supported the structure hung intricately woven rope hammocks. Hanging on other poles and laid out on reed mats, that were being used by women squatting on the mud floor, we saw the beautiful tightly woven baskets that we had come to purchase. The baskets ranged from sack like shoulder bags for carrying small babies to very large disks for sifting corn. All had complex traditional geometric patterns of intertwined dark and light natural grasses and reeds of many shapes and sizes. All were functionally designed for daily use in the pueblito.

The many presents we had brought with us for the men, women, and children were gratefully received and we were invited to stay the night. As darkness fell the oil lamps were lit and we sat around the smoky open fireplace eating porridge-like corn mush, some rather tough and stringy meat of unknown origin, and drinking very fiery liquor. At about 10 o'clock we were each given a hammock and bid good night. I struggled to fall asleep twisting my body into every possible contortion to find some modicum of comfort. I slept no more than a couple of hours and in the morning, exhausted and with a severe backache, was awakened by the early call of a rooster. After purchasing a number of beautiful baskets and shaking hands and thanking our hosts for their hospitality, we started our drive back. No problems crossing the Orinoco once again. The captain"greeted us like old friends and steered his raft-like ferry with great skill to dock at the village jetty.

I chose to drive. A few hours later, after a roadside picnic lunch, a beer, and feeling the soothing warmth of the afternoon sun and being lulled by the steady hum of our car on the paved road my companions dozed off. They too had had a miserable night.

I fell asleep at the wheel. The car left the road and landed on its roof. We found ourselves hanging in our seat belts but crawled out shaken but unhurt. The hatch back door had sprung open. Baskets were scattered for twenty feet around the vehicle. We had missed large boulders by a only a few feet. Twenty minutes later we flagged down two trucks carrying local road repair crews who stopped and ran over to the scene of the accident expecting to find the dead and injured. With ropes and combined teamwork they helped us right the station-wagon and drag it back to the road. To our surprise the engine started and after bending the front mudguards we were able to slowly continue our journey. Very late that night, after cautiously edging that battered station-wagon into the stream of fast moving traffic on Caracas' ever busy freeways, we arrived home.

Fifty years have passed and those beautiful baskets survived. They adorn the walls of my old Texas bungalow even now.

# 29. Filling In The Spaces

**Mia Sundby**

I've always loved old maps. I don't mean modern maps forgotten in car glove compartments, ones yellowed and cracked with age that creak when you open them, worn away at the creases and sighing open with drowsy excitement at the thought of being used again —the sort of maps that were folded away six years ago after that one particularly long car trip where they remained the only sane and silent travel companion amidst the sighs and stretching legs and snappy stand-offs for who could be in control of the radio—, though these veterans of family life hold their own charm.

I mean truly old maps, the sort painstakingly painted by hand in the sixteenth century, the ones that warned 'here be dragons'. Those are the maps I've always loved. Those are the ones with the blank spaces. There always seemed to me so much meaning to those spaces; it wasn't that the artist hadn't gotten around to drawing that yet, it was simply that no one knew what was there. In our age of information, of whirring wisdom and beeping beacons of communication, it's almost impossible to imagine not knowing what lies beyond the horizon. It's with a confusing combination of dismay and relief that I recognise that nowhere on the common map is there a blank space that a traveller might wander into, encountering who knows what. Earlier this year my best friend went to Amsterdam with her dad for her eighteenth. It was the first time she'd ever been on a plane.

On the day she set off, my phone buzzed and I flicked it open to see her message into our friends' group chat:

"Airports are weird."

I, a somewhat seasoned traveller with enough early experience of planes and airports for them to retain no novelty to me at all, laughed to myself and messaged her back. What ensued was a short conversation where she mentioned how overwhelming, yet exceedingly boring, it all was. She then messaged a quick goodbye as she was boarding.

And disappeared into silence.

As I sat staring at my smartphone, my key to a trillion troves of knowledge, I wondered if the spaces between communication are the only blank spaces we have left. With everything else filled in, is the only remaining mystery the silences between speech? You can't travel across that space just as you couldn't with so many of those empty areas on the old maps. In an era of evidence, where 'pics or it didn't happen' is a common phrase, is messaging after a significant amount of time the only mystery we have? In the same way that sailors would return, windswept, skin smelling of sweat and salt, and cry that they had seen something we wouldn't believe?

Two hours and five minutes later, she messaged, "That was fun."

And I knew she'd landed.

Four hours and eleven minutes later, she filled us in on the day's events. She lamented the amount of damage she'd done to her bank account in the span of four hours and then left again. Vanished into space. She checked in several more times to comment on things she'd noticed, little differences between the UK and her experiences in Amsterdam —a city I myself have visited and loved not only for the picturesque city scenery but also for the diverse history of its formation including violent tales of religious disagreements, rebuilding of places of worship, city expansion, and the canals' histories— one such thing she discovered being the shock of Bolognese-flavoured crisps. And better pot noodles, apparently.

Whilst The Olden Days lacked things like pot noodles and most countries still lacked even potatoes, it struck me that, in our own twenty-first century way, we weren't so different from sailors of the old-map days; one friend in the chat returned with his own experiences of better foods in other parts of Europe, and soon several of us were trading stories of our travels to Italy, Spain, Germany, and France.

Like a weather-beaten band of sailors sat around a tavern table, we exchanged experiences, told tales of things we'd seen, foods we'd sampled, and eagerly reimagined each other's stories. Together, we were filling in our empty spaces. It's a common misconception of older generations to think that my generation enjoys no mystery —that we Google anything the moment we don't know the answer. And, for trivial topics of conversation or out of curiosity, we do. But the instant stories are being told of lands we've never seen with our own eyes, we slurp our figurative tankards of rum, pull up our chairs and lean in to listen, to fill in our own personal maps. In truly old maps, those blank spaces seemed to capture something so inherently human; they seemed to outline not an area we didn't know but a stubbornly human promise that one day we would. Those blank spaces inspired storytellers and travellers alike to speculate and venture out to discover, to rewrite the signs that warned 'here be dragons' and instead ink in 'here be something different'.

Next year, I'm planning a gap year. My travels will take me far away from home and most of the places I've travelled before (France, Spain, Switzerland, Scandinavia, Germany, to list a few), to the country where everything wants to kill you, Australia, where I have loving family who are the exception to that rule, then to Japan and South Korea. In tribute to those old maps and warnings of dragons, I'm also considering a short stop in New Zealand, the set of Middle Earth. I've researched chunks of what I plan to do in each country, where I might stay, what I might see, where I might work, how I might volunteer, but I've left some gaps. Not because I don't know what to do with them, but because I will fill them in my own time.

I am both thrilled and terrified at the prospect of this journey, as I'm sure many sailors of The Old Days were, though thankfully I have a lot less mortal concerns (such as starvation, rats and infection), and also have the information-stuffed tomes of the internet in my pocket. And though Earth, as far as we're concerned, is filled in, and I am not part of some eccentric expedition to discover what lies beyond the horizon, I am, in my own way, setting out on an adventure to fill in the spaces of my map, to rub away the signs that say 'here be civilisation' and ink in 'here be something different'.Who knows… Perhaps there are some dragons left.

# 30. Navigating Yagoua
(A Town in the Extreme North Province of Cameroon)

**Honor Teodoussia**

*Cameroon*

## Leida Field on the Outskirts of Town:

It has been almost a year and still Yagoua spins around me like a maniacal kaleidoscope. I pass a field every day on my way to school that vaguely registers as some type of billowy black foliage growing on brittle bones. Then one day I see what it really is. Hundreds of plastic bags snagged on dry brush.

In a slap of clarity, everything clicks into focus. My Foulfoulde teacher pointing to a plastic bag. "Leida," he said. "Leida," I repeated. This is Leida Field. Plastic Bag Field. There is only kind of plastic bag in Cameroon. Black, thin, the weight of 10 tomatoes could split its transparent skin before you even get home from market.

Almost every structure in Yagoua is softly imperfect, made of mud, grasses, and twigs, with bits of sunlight peeking through little holes. The walls never meet the dirt floors exactly. Never more than semi-privacy created by thatch weavings called seikos. Everything lumpy, frayed, wood, mud, plant matter. The circle of life presents itself daily in the growth of plants that are then cut down, woven into walls, then quickly disintegrate and collapse back into the earth.

Amidst the perpetual browns that merge everything into a blur, I search for familiar navigational tools—a street sign, the hard edge of a building, a corner, a straight path clearly designated as such. A sandy footpath I successfully follow to a colleague's house one day is the next day forked differently and ends abruptly behind the prison.

Chad to the East; Nigeria to the West, Yagoua is a high-desert town 20 kilometers from Zebe, a river town in Chad that sells tilapia, sardines, and catfish. We make a run to the border standing in the back of a pick-up truck to get fish. On the return trip, with fish the size of dogs wrapped in brown paper and fibrous market bags at our feet, one of the standing passengers bangs on the top of the truck cab and yells "Ha do! Ha do!" The pick-up slows and lets that person off. From there all the way back to Yagoua, there's a Wild West feel as we bang the top and yell, "Ha do!" for other passengers getting off in the bush. I see only dusty plains with occasional acacia and baobab trees. I wonder where their homes are hidden.

Yagoua is 500 kilometers from Banki, Nigeria. We cross the border in a bush taxi at Mora into Nigeria. I buy two pagnes (cloth), a volleyball, some stickers, a bottle of rum, lotion, and conditioner. Goods are less than half price in Nigeria. We pass huge flatbed trucks, packed high and top-heavy like three story buildings. Tied to the truck's side slates are plastic teapots and casserole dishes big enough to mix a batch of beignets for an all-night party. The pots are white and painted with African leaders, flags, political slogans. The trip should take four hours but takes over six. We stop for prayers at 1:30 and 3:30 going to Nigeria and at 6:30 and 7:30 coming back. We stop at four military checkpoints going and six coming back to show our carte d'identites. The gendarmes are sour-faced and angry until they get a bribe and then there is laughter, promises of drinks next time, and As-Salaam-Alaikums for the Muslims. The passengers breathe easy and we continue our ride with a festive feel percolating as we get closer to Nigeria but a weary feeling on the way back.

## Hadja's House, East of Leida Field:

Hadja runs a successful water delivery business, is a landlord to two tenants, myself, and a couple from the South, and serves as a central hub of news in Yagoua. Before I came, Hadja hadn't left her compound for 13 years since she married and moved in. She's 29 years old.

Hadja had her first three children at home. Her fourth child she has while I'm asleep. This is the one time she leaves the compound—late at night, accompanied by her husband, and back before dawn. She hands me the new baby and complains that the hospital was dirty. The baby has a leather string with small pouches dangling around his perfect round belly. It's a protective gris-gris and I wonder when and how Hadja acquired it. Did a marabout come to the compound when she was pregnant? Did her husband go to the marabout while she was giving birth?
Do they sell the gris-gris at the hospital?

Hadja is not hindered by her seclusion. She considers it a privilege that she does not have to go to the market with the common masses. At least that's what she tells me. The market is paved with what look like cobblestones but are actually mango pits. At first the market makes me dizzy. Children hurtle themselves at me and frantically chant "Nasara! Nasara!" calling out my whiteness. The naked man rubbing garbage on himself then throws the garbage toward me.

I pay full price for an onion because it seems like an unnecessary use of time to barter for an onion. News of this affront reaches Hadja before I get back to the compound. She explains to me that I am being disrespectful for not considering the onion seller important enough to spend time bartering with him. Eventually I learn to start my market day at the bil-bil bar with a gourd full of millet beer. What initially tastes like goat piss becomes a delicious elixir that slows the spinning kaleidoscope and gives me the patience to barter for onions.

**The Market:**

Once I am conditioned to the market, it becomes a hypnotic place that holds me there all day. Hours are spent at Disco, an empty room save Aboubakar sitting behind a desk topped with a boombox and stacks of cassettes in cloudy plastic covers. Bring a blank cassette and Aboubakar will record the latest Bikutsi, Makossa, Bend Skin, and Zouk on it. Aboubakar is an intellectual on par with any college professor I ever had, so the hours spent at Disco are not so much for the cassettes as they are for the debate.

I visit Bouba. He has a plumbing atelier in the market. It is a shed with a few pipes and tools. He is a plumber in a town where there cannot be more than twenty homes with indoor plumbing. He is the best dancer in town. His specialty is "rock," which is 50s sock hop dancing. It is surprisingly popular in Yagoua. But so are the TV shows Dallas and Night Rider. Bouba's sister, Fatimatou, has a hair salon across from the BP station. She giggles when I ask her to try to braid my hair. She calls all her friends around and says, "Ca glisse!" They take turns but no one can make my "slippery" hair stay in braids.

The market is organized so all like goods and services are together. Vegetable sellers sit behind their huge silver tubs of carrots, onions, tomatoes, peppers. The carb section stocks millet flour, rice, beignets, potatoes stacked in impossibly tall pyramids on the ground. The meat is on tables and often covered with heavy cloth. I buy "fou fou," or cow lungs to feed my cat. It's the cheapest and really only choice after being shamed for buying canned sardines. I bought the sardines at the "White Man's Store." Bouba buys cocktail weenies at the White Man Store. I tell him they are made with pork, which he doesn't eat as a Muslim, but somehow this kind of pork doesn't count.

The fruit is small, misshapen, and packed with rich flavor that is nothing like our oversized, perfectly shaped American fruit that tastes like weak sugar water in comparison. Brochettes are chunks of roasted meat from longhorn cattle. Sometimes it comes with a small dab of the buttery fat from the cattle's hump. Whole roasted chickens are wrapped in brown paper with a tiny tightly twisted pouch full of red powder—the delicious and ubiquitous pimente—spicy pepper.

A nameless restaurant is a cinder block room with a slightly dug out, soft sand floor. The menu is on a chalkboard. Everyone sits together at the two long wooden tables with benches. Bouba orders Os Pain, which I confusedly translate to "Bone Bread"? Yes, bones full of marrow that he sucks out and bread to soak up the delicious broth.

**The Sand Hill to School:**

Most of the year, there aren't many insects in Yagoua. It's too hot. One day it is 113□ F. I lose hair from the top of my head walking to and from school twice a day up a steep sand hill that fills my flats moments after I empty them, which I do over and over all the way to school. My hair burns out of my head until I finally get a hat.

The sadly brief rainy season brings a bit of coolness but also the most oddly behaving flies. They ride on people's backs. You see someone whose back is covered with maybe fifty flies and you wonder if you also have a back full of flies. You flail your arms to check. You've now agitated all of your flies. They dive bomb your ears, buzzing in and out, in and out.

At the top of the hill, one woman sells beignets rolled in sugar. Another woman sells anti-crise, water mixed with lemon and sugar served in a tied-off plastic bag like a goldfish won at a carnival. You bite the tip off the full end and drink it down all at once. In the perpetual economic crisis, this drink offers a cheap option to manufactured and bottled drinks.

**Drinking Spots:**

The bil-bil bar where I fortify myself for market days is four thatched seiko walls, sand floor, squat stools in a circle around a big vat of fermenting bil-bil, and empty gourds scattered around. The bars in Quartier Sara are a step up. Some are like the bil-bil bar but many have mud brick walls instead of seikos and benches, taller stools, sometimes even an armchair or two. Drink selections include wine bottle sized super sweet soda called Top followed by the name of its flavor: Top Anana, Top Mangue, Top Orange, Top Citron, Top Soda. Top Soda is my favorite. It's like club soda. It is the only one that doesn't make my heart pound with sugar jitters.

Mama Campamount's is the next step up. Here you find Muslim men in bou bous, ordering "Coca Alhadji," which is code for Coke with whiskey hidden in it so the "Alhadjis" can drink without shame. Mama Campamount herself is a beefy, rough woman who runs her bar and the surrounding rentable rooms like a no-nonsense trucker. Her boisterous laugh and heavy hugs make me feel safe.

At the very top of Yagoua's nightlife ladder is Labamba, the boite de nuit, or nightclub at the end of town opposite Leida Field. To get to Labamba you have to go down a long wide sandy road that is lined with tall trees. In those trees alongside the deepest sandy parts are narrow trails left by the clandos trying to avoid getting stuck. Clandos are "clandestine" dirt bikes on which passengers sit behind the preteen boy drivers.

There is one deep spot with no room for side tracks. No matter how good your clando driver, you are bound to come to a slow stop in the deep sand and then just topple over sideways. Women wearing tight skirts sit side-saddle on the clandos so it is easy to jump off. There are always at least three clandos being pushed out at this sand trap. Pile-ups of fallen motorcycles and giggling Labamba patrons are inevitable on the way home when your legs are tired from dancing and drinks.

**Back Home to Hadja's:**

The houses and surrounding walls that make them compounds

are a mash-up maze of corrugated tin, seikos, mud and cement patched walls, car parts even. It's a complex weave that ends up a cluttered, clean, inviting neighborhood. Buttery light spills out from a door here, radio static sizzles there, wisps of laughter and talk float about.

I pass by Astajam's house where I watch and rewatch her four VHS Bollywood movies every weekend. I pass by Mamoudou's family compound. He is the smartest of my seven-year-old sixieme students who tells me that Bouba used gris-gris to get me to love him. I ask him what does it matter; love is good, right? Not when it's built on deception he tells me. Every day a little girl runs to me when I come home. She holds out her arms and I pick her up. She bubbles on in Foulfoulde, but I can only understand that she is as happy as the sun. Because of her, the neighborhood children see that I am not a white monster and they stop yelling "Nasara!" at me.

At the end of a long night in Quartier Sara, sleeping inside is unbearable. It is over 110°F, not just occasionally but almost always, even at night. My skin feels like wax and my body smells like expired milk and yeast. So I soak my pagne in cold water, put it over my body, and sleep outside. The wind blows strong but doesn't cool. It is heavy and warm and throws sand directly into my face. My teeth crunch sand, my face is gritty with sand, the quickly dried pagne is itchy with sand. A leida whips over my face. I cringe thinking about what might have been in the leida that has just brushed my lip. I teeter on the edge of wired sleep. Throughout the sweltering night, I throw the stalking leida off me three times.

I wake looking like a gingerbread cookie dusted with layers of brown sugar. I have a tremendous hangover. Ashamed, I drag myself inside and try to go back to sleep. Hadja is standing next to my bed. She tells me to sit up. I feel like a child who is about to get scolded. But she hands me a delicate teacup full of black coffee. This is shocking because in my almost two years in Cameroon, I have never seen anyone drink black coffee. Though Cameroonians grows high-grade coffee, it is all exported and rarely does anyone drink coffee made from Cameroonian beans grown in Cameroonian soil. They drink instant Nescafe with more sugar or sweetened condensed milk in it than coffee. The pitch-black coffee that Hadja gives me is sweet but rich and robust. I doubt I can get a cup of coffee down with this hangover. But with Hadja standing over me like a soldier, I gingerly take a sip. Then another and another. Before I finish the cup, I feel good. I am restored. The light, slipping feeling in my head is gone, magically replaced with a grounded, solid feeling. Everything settles into place.

# 31. Traveling blind

**William Thompson**

*The States*

Traveling blind is always a cross-country game of pass-the-parcel—and I'm the parcel. I am handed-off from one person to another, on and off planes, into and out of cabs, until, finally, I'm deposited in my hotel room at the end of the game.

As I get ready to leave my home, I pace—I prowl. I check everything around the house half-a-dozen times before calling a cab. Often, I'm doing this early—middle-of-the-night early. I call a cab, then stand on the step to smoke and wait. It will be hours before I have another chance to smoke. Cab arrives, and we're off.

It's twenty minutes from my house to the airport. Usually, the driver will help me inside the terminal; once inside, I'm looking for someone who works for the airline. I've already checked in online, but I need help through security and to my gate. I find a person, and the process begins.

"Can I just check your boarding pass, please?"

(I show my boarding pass.)

"Thank you, I'll just ask you to sit for a few minutes until someone is free to walk you through security."

(Guides me to a seat.)

"Don't worry, Mr. Thompson. It won't be long."

I wait. Everyone understands waiting in airports; everybody has to do it. But my waiting is overlaid with wondering—have they've forgotten me this time?

They haven't, of course. It's only my anxious brain on overdrive. At least, I'm smarter about traveling than I once was. Only carry-on luggage on these trips.

Retrieving luggage from the carousel at my destination airport can be problematic, especially when I forget the color of my bag. I managed this once flying to Glasgow. The burly Glaswegian helping me find my luggage kept hauling bags off and back on the carousel.

"Is this your bag? Here, have a look."

"No, not that one."

"Is this your bag?"

"Not that one either. It's...sort of a...duffle. I think it's grey"

I'm aware how unhelpful I am.

"Is this your bag?"

I reach for it. "Yes, thank god, that's my bag!"

A customer service agent arrives to collect me, and we are off to security. I show my boarding pass again, and the guard points us to the fast-line. I need three bins for all my stuff: the laptop, of course, needs its own bin; carry-on suitcase in the second; backpack, coat, and hat in the third.

The guard behind the conveyer checks my boarding pass, once again, then I hand over my white cane. Here, it gets tricky.

The agent aims me at the metal detector. Another guard tells me to walk forward and reach out my hand. I'm good at this—I hardly ever set off the alarm. I take the latex gloved hand and slip through the detector. No alarm.

"Now, sir, if you could just stand here for a moment, please."

And there I stand—caneless and more than usually vulnerable—while the customer service agent has her turn with the detector.

I think of all the names people have for my white cane. It's my lifeline—this length of rubber-handled aluminum that keeps me from harm. It collapses into four pieces, held together by a strong length of elastic, and I always fold up my cane before handing it over to security. People have called it a cane, a stick, a walking stick, a blind stick, and a seeing-eye stick.

(I like that last one the best.)

Once, an agent, upon retrieving my cane from security, asked me: "Can I please unfold your cane?"

"Of course," I said, with a laugh.

She held the handle and let my cane snap together. "I've always wanted to do that!"

The customer service agent is through, and now, it's packing up and off to the gate. In an ideal world, I would be happy to wander through the airport and head for my gate with ten minutes to spare. I could get coffee, maybe a cookie, and allow my anxiety to settle.

But I'm in the hands of this kind and efficient customer service person. I'm taken to the gate, shown a seat, and told that someone from the desk will come and get me when it's time to board.

Talking to and thanking these people is an important part of my airport experience. Those who move me around the airport go out of their way to be helpful: they are kind, generous with their time, and never in a rush. I'm always grateful for their assistance. And it doesn't matter the city: Vancouver, Toronto, Montreal, Charlottetown, Chicago, Glasgow, Auckland, Melbourne, San Francisco, or Portland. These people unfailingly get me through the airport unscathed and onto my plane.

Now, I'm at the gate. I sit, the package, waiting for my next currier. This is usually someone not at the desk, but someone there to assist anyone with special needs heading down to the plane. Most often, that's me, people using wheelchairs, and parents with kids.

■■■■■■■■■■■■■■■■■■■■■■■■■■■■■■■■■■■■■■■■■■■■■■■■■■■

Once, I was waiting to board a plane home. This precocious, nine-year-old kid was waiting with me. Apparently, the kid had been busy charming all the flight attendants. An airline personnel came to collect us, and she started talking to little Mr. Charming. The two of them walked away, leaving me sitting there.

I thought, "What the hell?"

I grabbed my stuff and followed them down the bridge and onto the plane.

Such things don't usually happen, but the customer service machine sometimes experiences a hiccup. I've been taken right out of the secure area by mistake; I've been shunted around, asked to wait here and there, apologized to, driven back and forth in the airport golf-cart, and asked many times if I required a wheelchair.

(I never require a wheelchair.)

But all are minor inconveniences. These people get me to where I need to go, and my appreciation is boundless. Their job is being helpful; my job is responding with patience and grace.

Once on the plane, I check my phone a last time, then start reading. A flight attendant finds me.

"Good morning, Mr. Thompson. My name is ———. Have you flown with us before?"

"Yes, thank you. Many times."

"Fabulous! Would you like a braille card that describes the safety features of the aircraft?"

"No, thank you."

Then follows a quick recitation on emergency exits, the fan, and the call-bell. All good. I always do my best to remember the names of these people on the aircraft.

I prefer the aisle, but I'm often in a window seat. Once, a young woman staffing the gate came to tell me that airline policy required anyone with special needs to take a window seat. She was moving me.

"Not that I mind moving," I said, politely, "but why is that?"

The poor young woman was immediately flustered. Someone else intervened, an older woman with the airline: apparently, people with special needs had to sit by the window in case of an emergency. Able-bodied people needed to sit on the aisle in order to assist others in need.

(I knew it, I thought. In an emergency, they'll sacrifice the old, the lame, and the blind while everyone else vacates the plane.)

I smiled and thanked the young woman, and, of course, sat by the window.

The flight passes, and I read. Once we land, I text my kids, and pass-the-parcel begins again: out of the plane, across the bridge, into the airport, and into a cab. I'm usually feeling nervy by this point—freeways, traffic, and an unfamiliar city all adding to my sense of displacement. Finally, the hotel. I pay the driver, hope to hell I can stand outside the doors of the hotel to smoke, then I venture inside.

I check in at the desk, and the last person in this chain of people takes me in hand. In a few minutes, I am in my hotel room, the door closed behind me, my ears ringing with the unfamiliar quiet, and my nerves twitching in the grips of an anxiety hangover.

I'm here, wherever I am, for just a few days. If it's a conference, it, too, will pass. Navigating the hotel, the conference, and the surrounding area is its own challenge.

Once my trip is done, I will experience the whole game of pass-the-parcel in reverse: cab, airport, plane, airport, and cab. At last, I will be deposited on my front step, a worn-out and crumpled package, exquisitely grateful to be once again in my own, familiar space.

## 32. Cuba After Fidel

**Tim Weed**

*Havana, Cuba*

At dusk on the evening of November 29, 2016, three days after the announcement of Fidel Castro's death, I set off on foot with a small group of friends to Havana's Plaza de la Revolución for a memorial rally attended by perhaps half a million people. It was not good planning but simple dumb luck that I'd booked a flight to Havana a few days after the revolutionary leader's death, just as the official mourning period was getting underway. I was determined to take advantage. As a frequent visitor to Cuba since the late nineties, and in light of the diametrically conflicting narratives surrounding the revolutionary leader's life, I've struggled to come to a satisfactory conclusion about Fidel Castro. This trip seemed to present an excellent opportunity to find out how the Cubans themselves felt about him—not the exiles celebrating in the streets of Miami, whose feelings were clear enough, but those Cubans who'd spent most or all of their lives in the society he'd presided over and shaped.

It was a comfortable tropical night and the Plaza de la Revolución, filled to overflowing with Cubans of every age and shade, buzzed with muted excitement. Groups of doctors stood together in their long white lab coats. Teenage school kids sat circled up on tarps spread out over the asphalt, some playing video games on their smartphones. Above the square, covering the façades of two government ministries, loomed the faces of Che Guevara and Camilo Cienfuegos, ten-story line portraits cheerfully lit up for the occasion like immense cartoon avatars of the revolutionary past. At the head of the square a spotlight illuminated the monumental statue of a seated José Martí, its Carrara marble gleaming ghost-like in the rapidly falling dusk. Above it all loomed the plaza's great obelisk, a three hundred and fifty-eight foot wizard's tower with a circle of red lanterns ringing its summit like a smoldering crown.

A line of dignitaries filed down to the stage beneath the statue, their forms casting tall shadows on the brightly lit marble. Oblong balloons bounced back and forth in the breeze above the crowd, clear rubber cylinders inflated to the size of rugby balls. Government-issue condoms, apparently; a longstanding tradition at gatherings like this.

A huge screen next to the stage began to project images, triggering a surge of excitement in the crowd: black and white film clips of Fidel as a young revolutionary leader in the Sierra Maestra; Fidel speaking at a huge rally; Fidel riding a tank as he directed the defense of the Bay of Pigs. The clips were punctuated by still photos, more recent and in color: Fidel with his brother Raúl; Fidel interacting with Cuban schoolchildren; Fidel conferring with Nelson Mandela, the Pope, Hugo Chávez. The crowd sang the Bayamesa. The eyes of the Cubans around me glittered with tears.

It wasn't a mob of wild-eyed idolaters. There were no displays of exaggerated grief, no unfriendly glares directed at American visitors, no feverish bouts of ideological nationalism. Even during the more provocative speeches I was struck by the dignity and restraint of those in attendance; there was certainly nothing resembling the whipped-up fury of a pre-election Trump rally, for example. Yet it was clear from the faces around me that the departed had been a genuinely beloved figure. The eyes of many of the attendees, young and old, especially but not exclusively female, were red-rimmed from days of crying.

Raúl Castro's speech was subdued, his bearing that of a mild-mannered octogenarian. Though he spoke with the guttural, expansive, r-rolling grandiloquence of a young revolutionary, he no longer possessed a young man's certitude. He exuded weariness, like a runner on the final leg of a very long marathon. It was a well-written speech though, and blessedly concise. Raúl listed some of the historic milestones he and his brother had lived through together, such as the day of July 26, 1959, in this same plaza, when Fidel had announced the agrarian reform law. The expropriation and redistribution of private property was an act that earned him the undying enmity of those Cuban and American property owners who'd formerly possessed most of the island's land. According to Raúl, it was a moment that felt like crossing the Rubicon, very likely sealing the demise of the young Revolution. Fidel insisted they do it anyway, to follow through on the insurgents' promise to redistribute the nation's wealth for the benefit of the poor majority.

There are thousands of Cuban exiles in Miami, Madrid, and elsewhere who revile that decision, and the man who insisted on going through with it. But here, nearly sixty years later, an immense crowd of Cubans had gathered under spotlights to partake in an emotional tribute to the same man. What was a traveler to make of it?


In two decades of regular travel to Cuba, I've spoken to many people with dissident views. I've yet to meet anyone with direct experience of being imprisoned for expressing their opinion, but I do have friends whose outspokenness has nearly cost them their careers, mostly at the hands of mid-level bureaucrats. It seems clear to me that in addition to his other qualities Fidel was an autocrat, intolerant of public criticism, and that this tendency has outlived him. Cuba is by all accounts a more free and open society than it used to be, but those who speak out against the regime—and those who push against the limits of the gradually loosening business laws—are wary of surveillance by fellow citizens and covert agents of the state. There are no legal opposition newspapers, and, with a few closely monitored exceptions, like the famous "Ladies in White," it's forbidden to organize or demonstrate against the government.

On the other hand, there's no question in my mind that Fidel dedicated his life, as a writer put it, to "batting for the losing team"—and there are many ways in which the legacy of the Cuban Revolution speaks for itself. In contrast to the state of affairs throughout most of the island's long history, education, health care, and basic nutrition are now taken for granted as inalienable human rights. The infant mortality rate is lower than in the U.S., and the elderly are treated with a respect bordering on reverence. The average Cuban is more cultured and better read than the average American, though vastly poorer. Due as much to civic culture and the Revolution's system of neighborhood organization as to the severe penalties that exist for violations of the law, the crime rate is exceedingly low; there is almost no gun violence, and little violent crime of any kind. Cubans find the relentless news of mass shootings in the U.S. incomprehensible—and who can blame them?

The Cuban Revolution, for all its flaws, built upon the country's rich cultural traditions to create a society where learning and creative achievement are prized commodities. Everywhere you turn you find stunningly accomplished artists, mechanics, athletes, doctors, engineers, and musicians. The fact that many professionals have to moonlight as waiters and taxi drivers is a bitter irony—but that doesn't diminish the extraordinary talent and accomplishment that permeate every level of Cuban society.

Americans bred to believe in the moral primacy of the free market may find the social victories of Fidel's Revolution pyrrhic, but it's important to observe that most Cubans I know don't see things that way. They're justifiably proud of their country's accomplishments in education, health care, culture, and athletics. Opinions on the broader state of affairs are more varied, but can perhaps be summarized by the words of Havana-based novelist Leonardo Padura:

"Cuba is trapped between two eternally competing visions. One is that it's a socialist paradise; the other is that it's a Communist hell. In reality, Cuba is neither a paradise nor a hell, but, rather, more of a purgatory, where some of us have the possibility of salvation."[1]


Plenty of citizens in Havana and elsewhere didn't bother to attend the crowded public memorials, choosing instead to work, sit on a familiar doorstep, stroll the Malecón, play chess, pedal a bicycle taxi, prepare a meal, or otherwise go about their business. Fidel's death came as a surprise to no one: he'd been ailing for

---

[1] As quoted in *The New Yorker*, "Private Eyes," October 21, 2013.

years and hadn't been in charge of the government since 2006, when he'd collapsed, on live television, at a public event.

Most Cubans, however, in neighborhood gathering places, private living rooms, and the eerily silent bars and restaurants (music and alcohol were banned during the nine days of official mourning), were glued to the dawn-to-dusk coverage of the funeral cortège reversing Fidel's 1959 journey from the Oriente to Havana, and conveying his ashes to their final resting place in a granite niche at the Santa Ifigenia cemetery in Santiago. The solemn motorcade was greeted in every city and town by thousands of mourners lining its path, and many of them were moved to tears. No one forced them to come out and pay their respects, and the overwhelming majority of the Cubans I spoke to—even those who are sharply critical of the government—remembered their former leader with a sense of affection and pride.

"Fidel won all his battles," a friend told me, smiling and shaking her head incredulously. "Every day you wake up and expect him to be there. But he's gone."

The anti-Castro celebrations in Miami were not covered extensively on Cuban state TV, but the details were available on the Internet, and the reactions of those I spoke with ranged from disgust to sadness.

"We may disagree," a friend in Cienfuegos remarked, "but it shows a lack of respect to celebrate the death of any human being, even if he's your worst enemy. When Kennedy died, even though it was only a few years after he'd ordered the invasion of our country by mercenaries, we didn't celebrate. We gave him due respect." In the end, my friend added, the unrelenting hatred in Miami will hurt those who choose to cling to it more than it will hurt Fidel. "You can hold out your thumb in front of your eyes and block a star," he said. "But the star will keep shining."


The morning after the big memorial rally, I went down to the Avenida de Maceo to watch the funeral cortège leave Havana on its multi-day journey across the island. People lined both sides of the Malecón with little Cuban flags in their hands—and in at least one case, mounted to a telescoping fishing rod. The motorcade was led by two olive-drab military jeeps, the second pulling a trailer with a miniature coffin draped in the Cuban flag. There were a few more vehicles, and a helicopter chopping the briny air over the esplanade, but that was it.

At first this struck me as anti-climactic, and oddly déclassé for the funeral of a man who was, love him or hate him, indisputably a major world-historical figure. But then I remembered that in life Fidel had consistently discouraged any cult of personality, discouraging statues, busts, and currency in his image, and forbidding the use of his name for cities, airports, or public squares.

As the motorcade drove past a man ran alongside for a moment, stopping to shout, "El Comandante vive en el corazón de los Cubanos!"

A woman in her sixties turned away, her cheeks streaked with tears, and another woman, robed in a long Cuban flag with a Fidel poster taped to her shirt, began wandering sadly away up the Malecón.

The people dispersed, the traffic resumed, and gentle waves lapped against the algae-furred coral rock beneath the seawall. Moments later, a single cannon shot rang out from the Cabaña fortress overlooking the city. And he was gone.

# 33. Full Body

**O. Alan Weltzein**

*Vietiane, Laos*

We shortcut through the Vat Mixay (temple) complex and enter the Lao Mekong Hair, Nails & Massage, on Nokeo Koummane Road in downtown Vietiane, Laos. The temperature hangs in the 90s in the capital, and we're due for the treatment our daughter, who works in Yangon, has promised for a long time. We shed our flip flops, don the proffered house sandals, and sip glasses of cold water as we sniff and select our oil. Wife and daughter opt for lemon grass; I go with lavender. I always liked lavender.

We climb the stairs, change out of damp shirts and shorts, put on the wide-mesh unisex low briefs we're issued, wrap in a towel, climb aboard the cushioned platforms: belly down, opening for nose and mouth between pillows. We lay on contiguous tables. Our daughter loves massages, especially here in Southeast Asia where a one-hour oil massage costs less than $20.00.

At a "Natural Springs Spa" an hour from home, the one-hour massage runs $109 and the "Hot Stone Massage," $129.

Sandals, a towel, low briefs, and low cost aside, my Protestant upbringing has not prepared me for this.

My parents, warm hearted, didn't make a habit of running their palms over my brothers and I after early childhood. I'd catch my father momentarily naked, once in a great while, in their bedroom or just after a shower. My mother never wore shorts after age forty-five or so, too embarrassed by her calves' bumpy matting of varicose veins. She passed her severe modesty on to her three sons. Except when applying makeup, she never sat before her vanity or lingered before a mirror. She didn't like clothes off unless you're swimming; in our house, as I doffed socks and shirt, just back from a run, she sometimes shook her head.

I grew up chubby, with too much body, and thought the best thing to do was keep it covered. Once I slimmed, after age eighteen, I felt less shame.

About twenty years ago in Istanbul, we vowed to have a Turkish bath. We'd crossed the Golden Arm into the Sishane district, walked uphill past the Galata Tower, but entering the 16th-century hamami on the women's side, my wife and daughter lost courage. I persisted, initially baking on a marble platform until my sweat poured. The paunchy attendant, with luffa sponges and a shallow metal basin or two, worked my body over.

And over.

I was laved. I trembled out of the gleaming hamami, a big white jellyfish.

Southeast Asia is not Istanbul. This would be hands on.

We'd received a foretaste of full-body massage just down the street from Melinda's apartment in Hledan Township in Yangon. Melinda patronized this beauty salon and figured we should pamper ourselves. At 9:30 in the evening, a comfortable 80 degrees or so, we three walked in for a shampoo. No cut, just shampoo. I kept trying not to act surprised that small businesses stay open after 10:00 p.m. A guy, long-haired with the usual slight build, took on my head. For well over half an hour he massaged, periodically working south to my neck and arms. His size belied his fingers' strength as he pressed and pushed and kneaded.

At home in the shower, my spread fingers rack my scalp for a few seconds. More like a quickie drive-through car wash. Neither my fingers nor anyone else's have ever worked over my scalp like this.

As the attendant moved away, my head awoke from a warm cocoon, my blond-gray-white hair lighter than ever, seeking escape. We emerged at nearly 11:00 p.m., having paid our 4000 kyet ($3.00) apiece. I walked about four inches off the pavement.

I didn't grow up with a religious tradition that allowed for such a shampoo. Other than overeating or masturbation, I didn't know much about this kind of thing. I don't fault my parents, who lacked both time and inclination. They would no more enjoy a massage than a visit to a hamami. I imagine they regarded massages as a waste of money and time. My father might have given it a go, but not Mother.

She would scoff.

I've been trying to unlearn their indifference to their bodies. A runner for decades, I stay more slender than they or my brothers have managed, and after it heats up, I like the sun on my skin. It matters that my legs have good muscle tone; that my calves bulge slightly. It matters to me. It's taken me a good while to outgrow a sense of indifference (tinctured with mild shame) about my body in all its particularity. I'm always happy to call it Protestant shame: our lapsed lot, covering up with more than fig leaves.

Upstairs with eyes closed, left cheek down, I listen for the masseuse's moves and barely hear anything except her hands. Both here and later, in two other cities, I repose in my body and concentrate on the masseuse's hands. She, always she, works silently, only whispering "turn over" or "over" in broken English partway through the hour. Left leg then right, then back and shoulders. My first masseuse starts with my ankle then works north, shaping my calves, kneading deep into my thighs. Her hands glisten with lavender oil, I imagine, as she works the dough of my toned flesh. No sags in my legs.

Her hands anoint me, a wave crashing, onrush then undertow, their pressure building up a pleasing heat. They approach the mounds of my buttocks, retreat from the edges of underpants and towel though I wish they didn't. Sometimes as she finishes her curving forth-and-back with both hands, she slaps them together just above my flesh, close enough to feel the air—applause to their work as though independent of the rest of her body. I learn to anticipate that soft slap.

After the oil, her hands work through a towel. She rubs down, in. My limbs heat, just slightly.

My long legs serve as warm-up to back and shoulders, where she bears down. Less than two thirds my weight, she pushes with the entire length of her lower arm, and at least once she squats on my back. She pulls down on the shoulders, rubs each vertebrae. My rib cage stretches and my back shimmers, each vertebrae a harp-string. She bends my arm, pulls back, and holds it momentarily in a yoga stretch like a kinetic sculpture.

After the soft command, I pull back from my drowse, heave around as smoothly as I'm able, keep eyes closed though I peek. I want to see her body as she works my body, watch her black hair curtain her face, her eyes. Bony shins and knee knobs, hard surfaces, prevent her hands penetrating, but the thighs invite her kneading.

And my stomach, much more. She uses round motions on this softest dough. Her fingers approach, recede from where my abdomen curves above my pubic hair. They play the edge of the towel draped across my hip bones. With my chest she rubs from inside out, stretching apart my breasts, and my nipples tingle. Her fingertips feather my ribcage, poise over my shoulders, and the softer sides above my kidneys. She avoids only my face and genitalia.

Her hands have made a pact with my body. I lay in a happy state, drowsed and aroused. I admit a clichéd male fantasy, wishing she would finish the job, fingers removing the towel, lowering those mesh briefs, rubbing my erection before her mouth opens, then her legs. This fantasy creeps close in my skin. But this isn't quite that establishment. I know better.

I have not embarrassed myself as the masseuse rises and quietly withdraws, oil bottle and towels in hand. She might have said, heavily accented, "All finished";
I say "thank you," forgetting to say Kob kun krub. Back in shirt and shorts, now less damp, I walk to the front room where we're seated and presented with cups of steaming tea, its warmth, coursing down throat to stomach, matching my skin's slightly scented glow. We pay, thank masseuses and clerks again, walk out into the wet furnace dazed into an awareness of our skin, ourselves.

This kind of hour could become a regular habit, as it has for our daughter.
In Luang Prabang, Laos, and Chiang Mai, Thailand, Melinda and I will again opt for one-hour, full-body oil massages.

One evening in Luang Prabang, as we ride our bikes back towards our hotel from the night market, we stop at another massage establishment that advertises "fish massage." Melinda has told me about this version of immersion, wherein one species of eager small fish, Garra rufa or "doctor fish" (i.e. toothless carp) nibble away at the dead or horny skin on the feet or ankles. At her excited prompting, I pay for the ten-minute special, remove my Tevas, and insert both lower legs into this pool, about 3' x 5', positioned at the entrance so that I (or whomever is receiving the treatment) become an object of curiosity and amusement, if not advertisement, for passersby. I've become the freak in a carnival sideshow, no barker needed.

I clutch a glass of soda but would prefer whiskey. I try to relax, imagine all the good fish lips accomplish, though I know this is no love affair with a young masseuse's hands. Sometimes the pinpricks tickle enough that I flinch. Sometimes, looking through the clear water  at the cluster of fish swarming my heels or toes, I immediately think "piranhas" and jerk. That diffuses the swarm but they're soon back and I resign myself. Afterward, as I quickly towel my feet, they shine slightly and I think cleansing thoughts—though subsequent reading suggests that some medical specialists warn against particular infections accruing from "fish pedicures."

In 2011, it was discovered that 6000 Garra rufa imported to the U.K. were infected with bacteria that can cause pneumonia, meningitis, or soft tissue infections. Not a good plan for anyone with any cuts or open sores or diabetes or heart conditions. The CDC in the States reports that over ten states have banned fish pedicures due to sanitation problems. During my quick session, I blink "the ick factor in ichthyotherapy": fish poop.

After a final surge of shopping in Chiang Mai's Warorot Road (Kad Luang) market, on my final full day in Southeast Asia, Melinda and I enter another massage establishment on Tha Phae Road in early afternoon. My wife and I are flying to Bangkok in a few hours and the next day, flying back to the States. It's the same sequence: selection of oils, removal of clothes, and eventually, hot green tea. This time I select the Thai Flower essence—my cutesy way of keeping a bit of Thailand on my skin, at least for a few hours.

This masseuse pulls limbs more than the other two. I lay on a floor mat, a loose dark curtain separating me from my daughter. We hear a couple of quiet sighs from one another during the hour. I can't get over the masseuse's soft motions coupled with her arm strength. My ears track more slowly than my skin as she hovers and shifts, an accomplished musician who plays my body. Afterwards, Melinda declares this is one of the best massages she's had (her attendant is male this time).

I know my skin won't remember her hands for long but in another respect, it does. It remembers this particular luxury of hands on. At home, where such a treatment exceeds $100, my pocketbook holds me back. I register that cost as an unwarranted self-indulgence. But in Southeast Asia I go for it, eagerly anticipate hands and fingers rubbing oil. I have long abandoned any residual traces of body shyness. After all, skin on skin remains, our most elemental contact, and in my youthful age I welcome massages—that lazy iamb that stretches out, rests tongue near lower teeth and narrows mouth, and promises intimate creature comfort.

# 34. Fear and Self Loathing on the Camino de Santiago

**Mark West**

*Spain*

*Day 1*

I wish God would've told me that it may not be a good idea to start a pilgrimage with a hangover. That's what I thought as I stood staring at a dirt path that wound its way up the Pyrenees and a 482-mile walk across Spain on a centuries-old pilgrimage route called the Camino de Santiago. Then again, I hadn't been listening to God much lately, or anyone else who had an opinion about my reckless behavior and apparent lack of rational thinking.

What sent me there? I guess the same things that brought me to my knees back home in Southern California- The dissolution of a 23 year marriage that taught me how to hate, the teetering of my first relationship after being separated that taught me how to love again, and a gnawing feeling in my gut that after more than half a century on this earth I was still lost, and would probably die with no better of an idea as to why I'm here than when I first stumbled into my mom's arms across a green carpeted floor in a suburb of Los Angeles more than five decades ago.

I was hoping that somehow taking a million steps down a path across Northern Spain in the middle of a blistering hot summer to find some saint buried at a church in a city named Santiago de Compostela would help me lose sight of some of the things I needed to rid myself of. I would leave those things behind with each boot print I made in the dirt and hopefully see the path that lies in front of me more clearly and figure out how to walk it with the time I had left before I shuffle off this mortal coil.

So, when I hit rock bottom, walking the Camino barged into my psyche like a bull running through the streets of Pamplona looking to gore a drunken tourist, and it wouldn't let go. I'd never even been to Europe, but with everything I knew and loved tumbling down around me, I didn't have to think twice.

"Thus, conscience does make cowards of us all, and thus the native hue of resolution is sicklied o'er with the pale cast of thought, and enterprise of great pitch and moment with this regard their currents turn awry and lose the name of action."

Hamlet


So, there I was, standing in St. Jean Pied de Port (literally "Saint John at the Foot of the Pass") France looking out at the Camino de Santiago and my future, literally and figuratively. Lao Tzu said, "A journey of a thousand miles begins with a single step." Yeah, well…I'll bet his first steps didn't take him 25 kilometers over the Pyrenees in the rain with a 30-pound pack on his back suffering from a serious hangover due to a "miscalculated cultural experience" the night before in Madrid.

Unfortunately, that momentary lapse of good judgment in Madrid had compromised my level-headedness and, more importantly, my sense of direction when I set out to take a train from my hotel to the central station where I could board my bus to St Jean Pied de Port. Not that my judgment had been stellar as of late. In fact, due to the shit bag of chaos my life had become during the previous year, my decision making was pretty much on the level of the dude who decided there should be 16 lifeboats on the Titanic.

After agonizing over the signs at the train station, I ended up heading in the wrong direction. Considering the state I was in, I guessed I was probably going to end up at the gates of Hell, or at the very least a Justin Bieber concert. And I figured I deserved it. Well, at least according to the hung-over voice in the back of my head who in his best moods thinks I'm as worthless as screen doors on a submarine. Best I can remember he went on to ridicule me and question how in the hell I was going to be able to hoof it across an entire country when I couldn't even navigate the Madrid train station.

Finally, after I turned myself around with the help of an older gentleman on the train who spoke English, I made it to the central bus terminal only to find the last bus to Pamplona wouldn't make the connection to St. Jean, my jumping off point for the Camino. I got out of line and kicked myself for the hangover, not planning, and for the gnawing feeling that this whole misadventure may have been a colossal mistake.

While I was wallowing in self-pity followed by a chaser of self-loathing, I spied a window for another bus company and discovered that they too had tickets to Pamplona, and in fact, their bus would get me there in time to make the connection to St. Jean. There's a saying that the Camino provides. Yeah, well, that kind of magic didn't exist in my fucked-up world at the time, but I took the ticket anyway and ran to catch my bus.

When I got to Pamplona, I found my way to the bus for St. Jean. At least where I thought it was supposed to leave from-my hangover infused insecurity was still questioning every thought and move I was making. Fortunately, two pilgrims were sitting on a bench (their backpacks tipped me off), so I approached them in the spirit of pilgrimatic kinship.

Kento was a short Japanese guy, probably mid- 30's, with a perpetual grin on his face. He was traveling, at least for the moment, with Asia, a mid-30's woman he had met in Madrid. Kento didn't speak much English, but he was animated, had a perpetual grin on his face, and kept bouncing up off the bench to make a point, although I was never sure what the point was. You couldn't help but like him.

Although I couldn't understand much of what Kento said, Asia was a different story. She was a beautiful brunette from Poland, probably in her mid-30's, and she spoke three languages fluently, English being one of them. We all boarded the bus which was only half full, and away we rolled to St. Jean. Asia and I talked for a while, but for some reason, she seemed a little guarded. Maybe it was because she was talking to a half-crazed emotionally bankrupt American with the scent of two-dollar a bottle Rioja oozing out of his pores.

She told me she was staying with an acquaintance in St Jean for two days so that she wouldn't be setting out on her pilgrimage the next morning, so I reasoned I wouldn't be seeing her again. After about an hour and a half on a winding road through the Pyrenees, the bus pulled up to St Jean in a drizzle. Asia and I hugged (she had told me she was a big hugger) and said our goodbyes.

Kento had volunteered to see if there was a room at his Auberge (the name used for many of the inns and hostels along the Camino catering to pilgrims), so I followed him past the center of town and up a winding, picture perfect cobblestoned street that crossed a river. It was almost too perfect.

We got to Kento's Auberge only to find it full. He offered me further assistance (I think!) but I shook my head no and offered him my hand, muttering the pilgrim's salutation of "Buen Camino." It was time for me to begin my pilgrimage, and to experience one of the primary reasons I had traveled halfway around the world- to be alone with the pathetic creature that had crawled out of the primordial ooze of my soul over the last few years.

The man whose self-esteem had been whittled down to a toothpick by an emotionally abusive marriage. The man whose guts had been eviscerated by a beautiful Swedish ex-model and mother of 4 who saved him and made him feel worthwhile, at least until she told him she no longer loved him. The man who secretly hoped he might find a cliff somewhere along The Camino that would make a fall seem like an accident.

After I left Kento, I walked down the cobble-stoned street under a steady drizzle alone, content to wallow in my over-indulgence-laced bath of self-pity. Not sure where to turn, I decided to walk back down the street and stumbled upon a room that was abuzz with activity. It wasn't an auberge, but it was a place one could obtain their "pilgrims' passport"-sort of like a real passport, with pages to get stamped in towns along the way. I had ordered one online, but it occurred to me that I had never received it.

After being issued my passport, I asked the woman who had helped me about a place to stay, and she directed me to one of the newest auberges in St Jean, just down the street. When I got there, I was glad to see they had beds. Due to the constant drizzle, I had become soaked and I pictured myself having to sleep outside and spending the first few days walking while coughing up phlegm and blowing snot onto the Camino. Not the best behavior for a pilgrim on some sort of spiritual quest I surmised.

I walked into town and got a bite to eat, the cafes were abuzz with activity- fellow pilgrims excited about their impending journey. I sat in silence as I wolfed down some Spaghetti Bolognese and returned to the Auberge. The proprietress offered me a French beer, and we talked a little about St Jean and the Camino as her husband watched some sort of Italian reality show. After she joined him, I wrote in her guest book- "Thanks for opening up your place and your heart to me."

No easy feat for a man whose heart had a fissure the size of the San Andreas Fault running through it. But the next day would prove that a few blisters, constant drizzle, and 20 kilometers of road that seemed like it went straight up (it got me thinking that somebody really screwed up on the directions to hell) would at least help me forget the sadness and pain that had sent me there in the first place.

# 35. Bristol Bay

**Keith Wilson**

*The Ocean*

The tide waits for no one. I don't know how many times I've heard Dad say it, but he's right. It's both time and tide, as the old adage goes, that wait for no man, but time and tide are synonymous, and they wait for no woman, child, flower, furbearer, or fish. I was never a stellar student, but I paid attention to the interesting parts — and as I understand it, gravity between the sun, our planet, and its moon pushes and pulls the ocean in a rhythm as reliable as night and day, summer and winter, spring and fall. It creates ebbs, floods, neap tides, and spring tides in a pattern that the rotation of a clock, the breath in a pair of lungs, or the beating of a heart could never match. The tide was turning before life existed, and it will keep turning long after we're gone.

Life on our planet began in the ocean, and it was the tide that washed it ashore. Then wind pushed microbes and flora above the shoreline, so seeds spread and bacteria colonized. Amphibians crawled onto higher ground and evolved into reptiles. Reptiles became birds and mammals. Now snakes slither after frogs, frogs feed on flies, and ravens scavenge for scraps. Great apes pick fruit dangling from trees. Species feed on one another, existing in one complex food web.

Meanwhile, life in the ocean has developed its own similar system. On the surface, fish leap and splash, whales spew faithful geysers, and birds swoop to scoop plankton and minnows. Beneath the surface is unfathomable and alien. It teems with great white, black-eyed monsters, mammalian torpedoes speaking in sonar, water-breathing exoskeleton spiders, and eight-legged monsters with the ability to change color and texture. In the darkest depths and deepest canyons, anglerfish navigate with flashlights from their foreheads. There are catsharks, seahorses, and lizardfish with illuminated skin. Mountains range from the North to South Pole, and life thrives at every level from the floor to the surface.

What separates land and ocean is the shoreline, indistinct and formless. The border between ripples and solid ground is ever-moving, ever-changing. It was only a matter of time before one of the land animals decided to push the boundaries. Some of the apes stood upright and walked on two feet and became people. We could walk and run farther than any other bipedal species, and we used the ability to exhaust our prey, club them to death, and have abundant sources of meat, allowing our brains to develop. With this development, for some reason, came ownership of land, trees, minerals, other animals, and even each other. We became obsessed with lines, and we drew borders between property, nations, and states.

Of course pushing beyond the shoreline was inevitable. At first, we waded, careful not to be caught in a current or eaten by something with big teeth and black eyes. Then we built rafts, kayaks, and canoes. We built baidarkas, boats, ships, and submarines. Vessels moved between continents, and people conquered and eradicated each other, using waterways as transport. We scoured the ocean, harvesting shrimp, shellfish, sharks and sardines, decimating populations. To people, the ocean was an endless void. Even now, after having left more footprints on our planet than any other species, we have explored less than five percent of the ocean floor.

The tide, however, washes away all footprints. It washes away a skeleton just as it washes away a tree branch. It washes away a village or a city the same as it washes away a sand castle. All the saltwater seas, are one mass of water, ebbing and flooding into each other — and as ice caps melt, high tide rises even higher. On the Pacific, there was once the land of Beringia, a conglomerate mass of what is now Russia, Alaska, and land between them. It was a barrier between the Pacific and the Arctic, but as the water level climbed, it was reduced to an isthmus called the Bering Land Bridge.

Before a time of seafaring, people hiked the Bering Land Bridge from Siberia to the Norton Sound, following food like mammoths, muskoxen, and antelope. Then the water level rose and the tide never again was low enough to allow forging from one side to the other. Surrounded by the rising water on either side, the Bering Land Bridge narrowed until the Pacific met the Arctic, and the land between Russia and Alaska was drowned by the Bering Sea. Now as the tide ebbs and floods against the shores of Russia and Alaska, Beringia is just another part of the ocean floor.

People spread in all directions across the Americas, separating into thousands of groups distinguished by customs, clothing, language, and their ancestral land as much estranged as the deepest parts of the ocean.

Some people stayed pressed against the Bering Sea — like the Yup'ik, the Unungan, and just some of the Athabascan. The Unungan settled along the Aleutian Chain, a string of tiny islands once the tallest peaks of Beringia. Maybe these Bering Sea people were left behind by people who migrated south, but I think they stayed on purpose to keep the Bering Sea and the treasures brought by the tide for themselves. They learned to harvest their sources from the sea with driftwood baidarkas, harpoons, hooks, and grass ropes. They hunted whales, clubbed seals, and caught trout, smelt, and herring. They had no system of numbers, no units of measurement, and they never had to worry about catching too many fish.

The Bering Sea narrows into a corner above the Alaska Peninsula and below the Kuskokwim mountains, where the difference between ebb and flood transforms the shore more drastically than the changing of seasons. This corner is an arm of the Bering Sea called Bristol Bay — where Naknek is nestled on the tundra.

The most abundant harvest from Bristol Bay is the salmon. Every summer, millions of them gather to Bristol Bay from the Pacific to fulfill their final purpose. The run, it is called. First, they mill and swirl in the saltwater like the spiral of a hurricane or the slow tick around a clock, each one waiting for the right condition in the tide. In schools and surges, they swim upriver, led by an acute sense of smell toward their natal lakes and streams. Beyond the brackish water, they forge against the current for miles, moving straight ahead to spawn, die, and continue a pattern in existence before the first twine was woven, before the first baidarka was built, and before the first human hand ever touched the water.

It was Yup'ik people who established the village of Naugeik at the mouth of one of these rivers flowing into Bristol Bay. They named the village after their word for a muddy place, where the tide climbs to cutbanks, distilling the sand into swirls and flows of thick brown. The Yup'ik were the first people to catch salmon there. They would filet and cook them or dry them over a rack in open air before saturating them in smoke of slow-burning birch and alder brush. Beads of oil dripped from deep red meat with a strip of skin\

Then Russians invaded in boats, mispronounced the name of the village, and it was put on the map as Naknek. In fact, they claimed all of Alaska as their property, and later they exchanged it with other invaders who had claimed another mass of land far to the south. They traded it for bits of paper and currency, a measure of invented value. People rushed to other parts of Alaska like Nome and the Yukon. Villages turned into towns of roughneck saloons and bearded sourdoughs.

Soon, people from everywhere arrived in places like Naknek, Egekik, Togiak, and Dillingham. Like the Yup'ik, Unguan, and Athabascan before them, they learned to work with the ebb and flood. They depended on them to launch sailboats, release nets, and catch millions upon millions of salmon. Canneries were erected, ports were constructed, villages sprouted into towns where salmon were caught, gutted, canned, and shipped.

The village of Paug-vik, on the north side of the Naknek River, was soon connected to King Salmon with a dirt path in the tundra. King Salmon was the site of an Air Force Base put in place during World War II. During the Cold War, it was ready and able to defend any sudden-second attack from the Soviets. With the advent of air travel and the King Salmon Airport, more newcomers flocked to Paug-vik than to Naknek, and Paug-vik was soon the new Naknek. The first Naknek, once Naugeik, is now South Naknek.

Meanwhile, , salmon populations were disappearing. Most people didn't know or care, but others wanted to prevent it from happening in Bristol Bay. Some of these people called themselves the Alaska Territorial Fishery Service. Like invading Russians, they were self-proclaimed. Unlike invading Russians, few people believed in their claim.

First, Alaska had to be called a state. Then the Alaska Territorial Fishery Service could become the Alaska Department of Fish and Game. Then their rules could be established and their suggestions could be put into practice.

Now, based on escapement, nets are allowed in the water during a designated time coinciding with the rhythm of the tide. It's not perfect, but it's an instance where people have learned not only to accept the ancient pattern of the tide and the annual influx of salmon, but to work with it. Alaska has one of the last, most sustainable fisheries on our planet because of an understanding of these cycles and patterns.

At the ebb on the Naknek River, the water is not much more than a trickle through ever-shifting mudflats. Skiffs and subsistence slope downward with the beach. Canneries reach out onto docks on top of crooked, splintering pilings. Drift boats tie together as a line of vessels stretching out into the channel. Flocks of seagulls gather, flapping and squawking, pecking at guts and grime from processors. Skiffs lay in the mud with the flukes of their anchors stabbed into the flesh of the beach, waiting for the flood to take them back afloat. As the water ebbs, pilings are like trunks of trees rising. Tributaries as thin as fingers trickle down the mud into what's left of the channel.

After the water has disappeared into the forever of the ocean, there are the moments of slack tide when no twigs, leaves, clumps of grass, or bubbles move on the surface. These moments are brief moments of stillness, but soon, as though a table were tilted, the tide begins to shift direction. It moves faster and faster, and white water gushes in over the mud flats, boats rocking and thrashing as the waves chop like madmen with axes. Pilings sink back into the water.

Outside the mouth of the Naknek River is the Naknek-Kvichak District of the fishery, where commercial fishermen are permitted to fish. Salmon swim into nets anchored between buoys placed there by netters like Dad and me. In the deeper water, they collide into nets floating behind driftboats where fishermen sleep in onboard cabins, fish in nets behind them. Aluminum and fiberglass hulls smash each other for the optimal spot at the border, where fish swim thickest. Cork lines splash with heads and tails on the surface. Corks bob from hits below it. Salmon are caught, delivered, processed, and disbursed to all corners of the continents — places where salmon used to return, and places where they may never have been.

Above the water, above the cutbank, most traffic downtown is comprised of cannery workers on foot, between meals at Peter Pan, Red Salmon, Silver Bay, or whatever cannery employs and houses them. They linger along the paved shoulder of the Alaska Peninsula Highway, traveling in packs, assorting themselves by the places they call home. There are Japanese workers with knee-high, gray, rubber boots, Ukrainian teenagers with dreadlocks and bandanas, white trash with neck tattoos and face piercings, mustached Mexicans blaring music from smartphones, and lanky West Africans appearing as tall as phone poles.

Fishermen linger out of Naknek Trading with plastic bags of Kraft Macaroni, cans of Bush's Baked Beans, and bananas as brown as the beach. They head back before they can fish again. People stumble off the steps of Fisherman's Bar, Hadfield's, and the Red Dog, hoping the money they've made this season hasn't disappeared into the Barmuda Triangle. Boxes of leftover pizza leave D&D Restaurant in cars, onto the backs of fourwheelers, held down by bungee cords. The aroma of grease and scraps attract tagless dogs wandering town like the silent homeless population they are.

By the end of July, the numbers of salmon taper and fade to the occasional splash or bob of a cork. Fishermen and cannery workers load planes taking off from King Salmon. Then there are none. Boats fill the boatyards and canneries board their windows. Seldom is a car on the road, and foot traffic is no longer people but the occasional dog or brown bear wandering for scraps. Off in the distance, a sudden shout or a gunshot might echo across town without question. The gate in front of every cannery closes, and Naknek is still, like the river in the moments between the change between ebb and flood.

500 or so people, half the population, stay in Naknek, picking berries, hunting moose and caribou, chopping firewood, and winterizing pipes. Many of these people are direct descendants of those who walked the Bering Land Bridge. Many of them are not. No matter their ancestry, all people who stay in Naknek watch yellow leaves fall from birch and alders as cold air creeps its way across the tundra like a ghost, leaving it brown and dead in its wake. The days get shorter. The nights get darker. The air gets colder. It will be months before the salmon return again. It will be months before the masses arrive into the King Salmon Airport. Meanwhile, out in Bristol Bay, the Bering Sea, and the depth and expanse of the ocean, the tide ebbs and floods as our planet and its moon orbit around the sun.

# THANKS TO OUR EDITORS

**M. Brianna Stallings** is a writer and editor, though she prefers the title "Professional Word Wrangler." She earned her MFA in Writing & Publishing from Vermont College of Fine Arts. She lives in Austin, TX. Brianna was our Guest Judge and Editor for 2019.
mbriannastallings.contently.com

**Sarah Leamy** is the author of the award-winning books *Van Life, When No One's Looking,* and *Lucky Shot.* She is the Managing Editor/Founder of *Wanderlust Journal* and Wild Dog Press. Born in England, she's lived in Europe, Guatemala, and the States, now making a home in New Mexico. Sarah is the founder and managing editor of www.wanderlust-journal.com.
 www.sarahleamy.com

*And thanks for the extra copy-editing help from:*

**Carley Fockler** is a full time Floridian and a writer working on her MFA in Creative Writing. She is the Editor-In-Chief of *Obra/Artifact Literary Magazine* and has been featured on their blog page. She has read her work in New Smyrna and in Ipanema, Brazil. Carley has published a short story in *Touchstone Magazine.*
https://belljarbeast.wixsite.com/carleyfockler/blog

# THANKS TO OUR CONTRIBUTORS

1. **James Agombar** resides near the east coast of the UK. He is an author of speculative fiction, but has been equally inspired by many travels around the world. <u>Read more.</u>
2. **Susanne Aspley** retired as a Sergeant First Class after serving 20 years in the US Army Reserve as a photojournalist with tours in Bosnia, Cuba, Kuwait and Panama. Aspley also worked in North Yorkshire, England as well as Ra'anana, Israel, and is now living in Minnesota.
3. **Anthony Bain** is a British writer and journalist living in Barcelona. His first travel book, Wanderings along the Camino, is available on Amazon.
4. **Michelle Bracken** lives in Los Angeles. "Being There" was previously published in Empty Mirror in 2017. Her work has appeared in Litro, The Baltimore Review, Forklift, Ohio, The Superstition Review, RipRap and elsewhere. She received a notable mention in The Best American Essays of 2016. <u>https://www.michellebrackenwriter.com/</u>
5. **Steven Brouillette** is the real thing. A heart and passion for community and family, risking his life as a wildland firefighter, he's a Chief, Squad and Engine Boss.
6. **Danny Burdett** has had poetry published in several journals and is the author of the film and travel blog, Pictureland. Mr. Burdett lives in Chicago. <u>https://themoviegoer-danny.blogspot.com/</u>
7. **Kaori Fujimoto** is an essayist and translator from the Tokyo area where she currently resides. Her writing has appeared in American literary journals and anthologies.
8. **Lindsay Gacad** is a poet and essayist with an MFA in Writing & Publishing from Vermont College of Fine

Arts. Her writing has appeared in 2 Horatio, Divine Caroline, Levitate Magazine and others.

9.  **Steve Gardiner** has published five books. His articles have appeared in The New York Times, The Christian Science Monitor, and many other places.
    http://www.quietwaterpublishing.com/

10. **Daniel Gabriel** is the author of four books, and a lifelong vagabond traveler who has taken camelbacks, tramp freighters, and third-class trains through over 100 countries.
    https://danielgabriel.us.

11. **JL Hall** is a Scottish writer whose essays and short-fiction have been published online and in anthologies. In 2009, she completed a solo round-the-world trip. My Name Is Mai was originally published on www.imustbeoff.com. www.jlhallwriter.com

12. **Rebecca Hart Olander**'s first chapbook is forthcoming from Dancing Girl Press in 2019. She is editor/director of Perugia Press.
    rebeccahartolander.com

13. **Greg Hill** is a math tutor, adjunct professor of English, and voice-over actor in West Hartford, Connecticut.
    gregjhill.com

14. **Robert Kunzinger** has published eight volumes of essays, including the critically acclaimed Penance and Out of Nowhere. He does his non-traveling in Virginia.

15. **Wendi Kozma** teaches English at Marshall University in Huntington, WV. Her work has previously appeared in The Ship of Fools and Flash Fiction Magazine.

16. **Karen Lethlean** was born in Perth, Western Australia. She currently lives on the other side of the wide brown continent in Sydney. A writer, teacher, and athlete, she has completed the Hawaii Ironman triathlon twice.

17. **Frank Light** has published adaptations from the draft memoir Adjust to Dust: On the Backroads of Southern Afghanistan, from which this essay draws, in multiple literary journals and anthologies.

18. **Bridget A. Lyons** is a writer, editor, and explorer living in Santa Cruz, CA. www.bridgetalyons.com

19. **Dheepa R. Maturi** is an Indian-American writer living in the U.S. Her essays have appeared in Entropy, the Brevity blog, Tweetspeak, Dear America, and elsewhere. www.DheepaRMaturi.com

20. **Devan McNabb** is a 24 year-old Michigander who loves life and the outdoors. A recent undergraduate, he's been moving in several different directions in hope of finding something that fits, at least for the moment. He decided to settle down in Mackinaw City, Michigan and his current adventure is trying to do the whole pay-the-rent-thing and see what staying in one place can teach him.

21. **Kari Nielson** has worked as a guide and land manager. Her writing has appeared in The Esthetic Apostle and Waymaking. She lives in the U.S.

22. **Paul Perilli** has recently published in The Transnational, Numero Cinq, Thema, Overland, Adelaide Literary Magazine, Blue Cubicle Press and elsewhere. He lives in Brooklyn, NY.

23. **Anitha Devi Pillai** (PhD) is an applied linguist and teacher educator at Nanyang Technological University (Singapore) where she teaches courses on writing theories and writing pedagogy.

24. **Anna Reid** lives in Nashville, Tennessee with her Scottish husband. She is working on a memoir, Prone to Wander. www.annareid.me. ("Gravity" was originally published in Claudius Speaks.)

25. **Harriet Riley** is a freelance writer focusing on creative nonfiction. She teaches creative writing. She and her Australian husband now live in New Orleans.

26. **Shelli Rottschafer** teaches at a small liberal arts college in Grand Rapids, Michigan. She is an outdoor enthusiast who embraces her journey, and documents it through poetry and creative nonfiction.

27. **Jonathan Sapers** is a freelance journalist and fiction writer in New York City (www.sapersink.com) who is lucky in family vacation places.

28. Born in South Africa, **Jonathan Smulian** now lives in Texas. As an urban planner, he has worked in 26 countries and wandered in many more.

29. **Mia Sundby** is a college art student living in the United Kingdom. She divides her time between drawing, college, a part-time job, nerd-ing and writing.

30. **Honor Teodoussia** sifted the description of Yagoua out of her molded, warped journals from 1990-1993. She now works for National Geographic Learning and writes of travels with her two Cameroonian-American children. https://travelwritingaway.blogspot.com/

31. **William Thompson's** essays and stories have appeared in both North America and the UK. He lives in Canada. http://www.ofotherworlds.ca./

32. **Tim Weed** is the author of two books of fiction. He teaches as part of the Newport MFA in Creative Writing at Salve Regina University, and is the cofounder of the Cuba Writers Program.

33. **O. Alan Weltzien,** English professor, has lived in Montana (USA) for over a quarter of a century. He's published two chapbooks and nine books, and loves traveling more than anything.

34. **Mark West** resides in California and was a happily married husband and father until his life crashed and burned, so he booked a flight to Europe and walked across Spain and wrote about it in order to heal. www.markwestwriter.com

35. **Keith Wilson** grew up in Naknek, a remote Alaskan fishing town on the coast of Bristol Bay, where he returns every summer for the salmon season. He has been working as a commercial fisherman for 23 years, but has also worked as a teacher in both the public school setting and as a TEFL teacher in Guatemala.

Explore.
Connect.
Listen.
Write.
Photograph.
Share.
Inspire.
Submit!

www.wanderlust-journal.com

Made in the USA
San Bernardino, CA
03 May 2019